Woman's Day
COOKING FOR TWO

From the Editors of Woman's Day

Woman's Day
COOKING FOR TWO

 Random House • New York

Library of Congress Cataloging in Publication Data
Main entry under title:

Woman's day Cooking for two.

Includes index.
1. Cookery. I. Woman's day. II. Title: Cooking
for two.
TX652.W67   641.5'61   75-34207
ISBN 0-394-49843-7

Manufactured in the United States of America
9 8 7 6 5 4

Illustrations by Jan Gerding

CONTENTS

Woman's Day
COOKING FOR TWO

INTRODUCTION

This cookbook is, of course, for newlyweds and for people whose children have grown up and left home—and for the many others who also cook for two, some on a regular basis and some just occasionally. They know, as does anyone who has tried it, that cooking for two has unique problems and advantages that require special recipes and instructions.

Whether it be an elegant, candlelit dinner, an impromptu lunch for an unexpected visitor, a simple supper for mother and child or the cooperative effort of two roommates in an apartment or dormitory kitchen—cooking for two need not be wasteful or monotonous, as so many people fear. It *is* possible to cook a variety of "real" foods in very small quantities, without waste or miscalculation. It is also possible to prepare certain things in large quantities and make thrifty, imaginative use of the leftovers.

Cooking for two requires a special repertoire. In many instances you cannot take a recipe for six and merely divide it by three. The proportionate amounts of liquids or seasonings may have to be changed. The cooking time may differ. You may need special kinds of utensils. Some recipes just won't work at all for two people: the "chemistry" of yeast or baking powder may go awry or certain ingredients will not be available in small quantities or will not taste the same when you use less of them.

The recipes in this book have been developed and tested by *Woman's Day* to meet a variety of needs and circumstances that arise when you are cooking for two. We have tried to adapt many of the favorite dishes of our readers to the special needs of small servings, and where that was not possible, we invented special dishes.

The Advantages of Cooking for Two

Anyone who knows what it's like to cook for large groups of people can see the special advantages of small-scale cooking. First of all, there is less work: fewer vegetables to peel or cut up, less meat to trim, season or brown. There is less marketing before the meal and fewer dishes to wash when it is over.

And you'll have more time to fuss with the appearance of a dish, with table settings and flowers that will make the meal more festive. You can make "fancy dishes" that are time-consuming to prepare in quantity, but quick and easy for two. You can make dishes which require last-minute attention—an omelet for two or some deep-fried Chicken Kiev—without having to stand chained to the stove like a short-order cook, turning out more food while everyone else is eating.

Because it is less expensive when you buy small quantities, you can splurge once in a while and treat yourself to the kind of luxuries that might be out of the question for large-family dinners. Scallops for two, for example, are costly but not prohibitive, and a splash of good wine in a sauce for two will not be missed from the bottle which later accompanies your meal. You can also afford to buy special accessories for the table: two cut-crystal wine goblets, for example, or a special kind of bowl or dish exactly right for the food you are serving.

SAVING TIME AND AVOIDING WASTE

How much to make—a frequent problem when you are cooking for two—is dealt with specifically in appropriate places throughout this book, both under the various chapter headings and in the recipes themselves.

In general, we advise preparing exactly what you need for two. There are exceptions, however: certain large cuts of meat can be used in a variety of "leftover dishes" (see *Menu Planning and Marketing*, below), and if you have space, you may wish to save time by cooking double quantities of dishes that freeze well, for future use.

You can also save time by making larger quantities of foods that keep well in the refrigerator and are good to have on hand: a batch of hard-cooked eggs, for example, or a cup or two of salad dressing.

Try to avoid waste by keeping evaporated or instant nonfat milk on hand rather than fresh milk, which may spoil. If you should need only half an egg for a recipe, beat the whole egg, measure out half and save the rest for when you next make French toast or omelets. Buy bread in small quantities. Many bakers will sell you half a loaf if you ask for it; bread also keeps well in the freezer. If your bread *should* become stale, however, pulverize it in the blender or with a rolling pin and use it as bread crumbs.

MENU PLANNING AND MARKETING

Menu planning in advance is highly recommended when you are cooking for two. It will cut down on the number of trips you make to the market and will help avoid wasteful leftovers.

Menu planning is particularly important if you decide to cook a large cut of meat—a roast or turkey, for example —on a weekend or when you are entertaining. There are many dishes which call for cooked meat or poultry: plan ahead for the leftovers and buy all of the ingredients that you will need to make easy and imaginative use of them. Each major recipe in the section "Large Cuts of Meat" is followed by a number of such suggestions. The planned use of leftovers will save both money and time; it should be part of any cook's basic strategy, especially one who is cooking for two.

If you have become accustomed to cooking for a large family and are now cooking for two, you will have to re-scale your thinking when you market. Five-pound bags of potatoes or large cans of fruits or vegetables are not necessarily economical—not if they spoil or take up room in the pantry that could be better used for other purposes. Don't be embarrassed to ask for small quantities of things. Try to get to know the meat man or the produce man in your

favorite market; they are often willing to break up packages of meat or vegetables for someone they know and in
many localities the law says they must.

Buy canned goods in small (usually 8-ounce) sizes to
avoid waste. Look for small onions and green peppers, and
for garlic heads with small cloves. Buy coffee beans and
grind them yourself in small quantities; ground coffee
loses flavor when it is stored too long.

If you buy perishables in small amounts, you will have
more room to store staples that keep indefinitely and are
cheaper when purchased in large quantities, and cooking
will be less harried and more enjoyable if you keep a good
variety of staples on hand.

Freezing

Good freezer space is a wonderful boon when you are
cooking for two. You can make double quantities of your
favorite dishes, freeze the half that you don't use and have
complete meals on hand when you need them. Freeze
cooked foods in portions for two. Try to use containers
that will be convenient when you wish to reheat the food.
Casserole-type dishes should be frozen in aluminum or
glass containers that can be taken right from the freezer,
put directly into a preheated oven and then brought to the
table for serving. Such containers are inexpensive and convenient; it pays to invest in several sizes. Do not use them
directly on the top burners or under the broiler, however,
unless the instructions for use say you can.

Cooked foods can also be packaged in freezer bags that

can be submerged in boiling water when you are ready to reheat the food. This procedure is especially good for foods that might dry out in oven reheating.

Use clean coffee cans with tight-fitting lids or good, heavy-quality plastic containers for freezing soups and stews. Such sturdy containers can be put in a few inches of boiling water to speed up defrosting and will not collapse in the process. Once the food in the container has loosened, it can be transferred to a covered pot for slow reheating.

Package uncooked meats in quantities for two before you freeze them. Wrap them in heavy-duty aluminum foil or heavy-weight plastic wrap; both are easier to use than freezer paper and equally satisfactory. Shape ground meat into hamburger patties and freeze them individually. If you have leftover cooked meat, slice it and package it in convenient portions. Very small quantities of foods like egg whites or sauces or small quantities of stock may be frozen in individual ice-cube trays or in small paper cups, covered with aluminum foil and secured with a rubber band.

The temperature of the freezer should be 0° F. or lower. Keep the freezer well organized and do not lose track of what you have there. Try to use the things that have been there longest, so that the contents of the freezer continue to rotate.

Prepare food for freezing with care. Remember that rectangular containers take up less space than round ones. Pack the food tightly in the containers, pressing to eliminate air bubbles. Food expands when it is frozen, so leave some space at the top. Seal the containers well and label them with a piece of tape, giving the date, the contents and the quantity. Use masking tape for labeling instead of freezer tape; it is less expensive. Write with a waterproof marking pen or with crayons.

When you are reheating frozen foods in the oven, you will usually want to keep the temperature at 325° to 350° F. Bring the food only to serving temperature; do not overcook it. Keep food covered while reheating, unless you want it to be crisp.

Try using a double boiler to reheat foods that might easily dry out in the oven. You can set up a makeshift double boiler, if necessary, by putting a pie plate over a pot of boiling water and covering it with another, inverted pie plate.

If you are reheating small quantities, it will be cheaper to use electrical appliances rather than the oven. Toaster ovens, slow cookers or electric skillets will do the job.

Equipment

Every kitchen should be checked and streamlined periodically. We all tend to collect things that are little used, take up valuable space and cut down on efficiency: it's a good idea, every so often, to get rid of the gadgets and utensils you haven't used in years or to store them out of your way.

If you are cooking for two after years of cooking for a larger family, you may have equipment that is oversized for your present needs. You may find you have less need for a large electric mixer, for example; store it where it won't take up valuable work space. A good whisk and a copper bowl are sufficient for beating up an egg white or two or a little bit of cream, and a portable hand mixer or a rotary beater will take care of many baking needs.

Cooking for two requires appropriate small-scale equipment. Although you can buy things like small baking pans and loaf pans in aluminum foil, if you cook for two on a regular basis, it pays to invest in sturdier utensils.

You will need several small saucepans, in 1-quart and 2-quart sizes, and small- and medium-sized skillets. A Teflon pan is especially useful for reheating leftovers. You will also need a large pot for boiling corn, cooking spaghetti and, of course, for when you have guests. As we have mentioned, a small double boiler is particularly handy when you are cooking for two; it's the best way to reheat small quantities of food and to keep food warm without letting it dry out as it would over direct heat.

It is good to have several small baking dishes in 10-ounce, 16-ounce and 20-ounce sizes that can go straight from the freezer to the oven to the table, so that dishes you've prepared ahead and frozen can be popped into the oven at a moment's notice. Inexpensive, heat-proof glass dishes with covers are very satisfactory for this purpose, as are those available in many other attractive and useful materials. A 1-quart casserole or soufflé dish and two individual 12-ounce ramekins should complete your supply of baking and serving dishes.

Individual custard cups and tart pans are very convenient for desserts. "Baby loaf pans," cookie sheets and muffin pans are also handy. If you fancy cakes and pies, it may be worth a trip to a bakery supply store to find 6-inch layer pans and pie pans small enough for two.

In addition to these basics, look over the following list

and use it as a guide when you equip or re-equip your
kitchen. Buy only those things that you are sure you'll use,
and add others as you need them. A well-equipped kitchen
is essential for carefree cooking, but the actual equipment
will vary according to the kind of cooking you do: some
people do very well without a meat grinder, for example;
others would be lost without a springform pan. The following list, although very basic, is intended just for
guidance:

- two or three sharp knives in different sizes
- bread knife
- knife sharpener
- cutting board
- wooden spoons
- metal spatula
- slotted spoon
- two-tined fork
- ladle
- rubber spatula
- one or two sets of measuring spoons
- measuring cups (one-cup and two-cup sizes)
- kitchen scissors
- strainer
- apple parer and corer
- grapefruit knife
- juicer
- potato masher
- grater and shredder
- can and bottle openers
- colander

- cheese grater
- funnel
- tongs
- pepper mill
- salt shaker
- containers for spices and herbs
- garlic press
- corkscrew
- rolling pin
- meat and poultry thermometer
- electric blender or food mill
- small portable timer
- small coffee pot
- large thermos to hold several batches of coffee when entertaining

The next time you prepare a meal for two, whether you are cooking for your husband, your child or a friend, make the most of the occasion. We hope that Woman's Day *Cooking for Two* will help you discover that cooking on a small scale can be a rewarding and exciting experience.

APPETIZERS
and SALADS

An appetizer is an invitation to dine, a hint of good things to come. The portions should be small, to encourage appetites rather than satisfy them.

Since the dishes in this section will be used most frequently as first courses or as side dishes, the quantities given are very small. You may, however, double some of these recipes, such as Fish-Cucumber Salad, Rumaki, or Curried Eggs, and serve them as a main course for lunch. You can also create your own unusual lunch by making small portions of several appetizers, like Deviled Eggs, Pickled Mushrooms and Fennel Parmigiana, and serving them together.

Some of the salads, such as Tomatoes with Green Sauce or Guacamole Salad, make good appetizers. Others, such as Rice-Vegetable Salad or Sweet-Sour Bean Salad, are best served as side dishes with fish or meat. Hearty salads like the Antipasto and Chef's Salad can be served as appetizers or as luncheon dishes.

Zucchini-Cheese Dip

½ cup (about ¼ pound) unpeeled diced zucchini
2 teaspoons chopped onion
¼ cup chicken broth
⅛ teaspoon salt
2 ounces cream cheese, at room temperature

Combine the zucchini, onion, broth and salt in a saucepan, and bring mixture to a boil. Lower the heat and simmer, covered, for about 10 minutes, or until the zucchini is tender.

Put the mixture in a blender, add the cream cheese and blend at high speed until dip is smooth. Chill until serving time.

Serve the dip in a small bowl surrounded by crackers, toast squares or raw vegetables for dipping. You will have about ¾ of a cup.

Rumaki

Here is an excellent way to use the liver that comes with a chicken. Freeze the liver and save it until you have two, enough to make rumaki. This dish is usually made with water chestnuts, but you can use apple slices instead, since water chestnuts are not usually available in very small quantities.

2 chicken livers, quartered

8 water chestnuts or ½ apple, peeled and cut into
  8 wedges

4 slices bacon, halved crosswise

¼ cup soy sauce

¼ cup sherry

1 teaspoon brown sugar

½ teaspoon powdered ginger

Put a piece of chicken liver and a water chestnut or apple slice together. Wrap them with a piece of bacon and secure the bacon with a toothpick. Mix the soy sauce, sherry, sugar and ginger in a bowl. Add the wrapped chicken livers and refrigerate them, turning occasionally, for several hours.

Remove the livers from the marinade and grill them under the broiler, or put them on heavy foil with slits cut in it and grill over white-hot coals. Turn them occasionally and baste with the marinade until they are golden brown, for about 10 to 20 minutes. Remove the toothpicks before serving them.

Serve the rumaki as an appetizer, or double the recipe and serve it for lunch with brown rice and a green salad.

Deviled Eggs

2 warm hard-cooked eggs
Pinch of salt
Dash of Worcestershire sauce
Pinch of dry mustard
¼ teaspoon lemon juice
About 1½ tablespoons plain yogurt or sour cream
Paprika

Slice the eggs in half lengthwise. Remove the yolks and mash them in a small bowl, adding salt, Worcestershire sauce, mustard, lemon juice and enough yogurt to achieve a smooth texture when thoroughly mixed.

Fill the egg whites with the mixture, dust the tops with paprika and chill them. Serve as an appetizer, with a few sprigs of parsley or some cucumber slices.

Deviled eggs go well with other appetizers as a main course for lunch.

Curried Eggs

2 hard-cooked eggs, quartered
3 tablespoons butter or margarine
2 tablespoons soft bread crumbs
1 tablespoon flour
½ teaspoon curry powder
½ cup milk or cream
Salt
Freshly ground pepper

Put the eggs in a small, shallow buttered baking dish. Melt the butter in a saucepan, remove 2 tablespoons and mix with the bread crumbs. Blend the flour and the curry powder with the butter remaining in the pan and cook over low heat for a minute or so. Stir in the milk slowly and cook, stirring, until the mixture has thickened. Season with salt and pepper to taste.

Preheat the oven to 350° F.

Pour the sauce over the eggs. Sprinkle them with the buttered crumbs. Bake for about 15 minutes, or until the bread crumbs are golden. Serve hot as an appetizer, or double the recipe and serve the eggs for lunch.

Fennel Parmigiana

Fennel, also known as finocchio, is sold in Italian grocery stores and can be found more and more frequently in other markets as well. Its anise flavor is fresh and unusual.

1 head fennel
Salt
Freshly ground pepper
2 tablespoons butter or margarine, melted
⅓ cup freshly grated Parmesan cheese

Trim the green tops and tough outer stalks from the fennel. Trim the base and cut the fennel from the top to bottom in slices about ¼-inch thick. Cook the slices in boiling water for about 5 minutes, or until they are tender. Drain them and season with salt and pepper.

Preheat the oven to 425° F.

Place the fennel slices in a small shallow buttered baking dish. Pour the melted butter over them and sprinkle with the cheese. Bake for about 10 minutes, or until the fennel is heated through and the cheese has melted.

Serve this dish first, as an appetizer, or combine it with other appetizers for an interesting lunch.

Pickled Mushrooms

Mushrooms, being rather expensive, are among the delights you can afford to buy if you are only buying for two.

½ small onion, finely chopped
1 small clove garlic, minced
¼ cup chopped parsley
1 small bay leaf
Pinch of pepper
¼ teaspoon thyme
¼ cup dry white wine
¼ cup white vinegar
½ cup olive or vegetable oil
2 teaspoons lemon juice
¼ teaspoon salt
½ pound small fresh mushrooms, washed and trimmed

Put all ingredients except the mushrooms in a saucepan and bring them to a boil. Add the mushrooms and bring the liquid back to a boil. Lower the heat and simmer, covered, for 10 minutes. Chill the mixture for at least 2 hours. (You can keep this mixture in the refrigerator for a week or more, if you wish.)

Before serving, remove the bay leaf from the marinade, drain the mushrooms and set the marinade aside to use as a base for salad dressing. Serve the mushrooms as an appetizer with sprigs of watercress or as a side dish with meat, poultry or fish.

Marinated Chickpeas

1 can (11 ounces) chickpeas, drained
1½ tablespoons minced red or green onion
1 tablespoon minced parsley
2 tablespoons vegetable oil
1 tablespoon wine vinegar
Salt
Freshly ground pepper

Combine the chickpeas, onion, parsley, oil and vinegar in a mixing bowl and toss well. Season to taste with salt and pepper. Cover and refrigerate, overnight or longer.

Serve the chickpeas as an appetizer on a bed of watercress.

Stuffed Vegetables

This is a nice way to use leftovers. Our Basic Filling works well with four different vegetables; recipes for each are given below.

Basic Filling
¼ cup chopped onion
¼ cup chopped celery with leaves
About 2 tablespoons butter or margarine
1 to 1½ cups soft bread cubes
½ cup chopped cooked meat or poultry or finely flaked cooked fish
¼ teaspoon salt
¼ teaspoon thyme leaves, crumbled
⅛ teaspoon pepper

STUFFED TOMATOES

2 firm ripe tomatoes

Slice off the tops of the tomatoes and scoop out the pulp. Chop the tops and the pulp and press out the excess liquid. Sauté the chopped tomato with the onion and celery in melted butter for 2 or 3 minutes. Toss the mixture with the bread cubes, meat (or fish), salt, thyme and pepper.

Preheat the oven to 375° F.

Put the tomato shells in a small shallow baking dish or pie plate and fill them with the stuffing. Bake the tomatoes for about 25 minutes. Extra stuffing can be baked in the same dish.

Serve hot or at room temperature.

STUFFED GREEN PEPPERS

2 green peppers

Cut the tops off the peppers, remove the seeds and membrane, and parboil the shells in boiling salted water for about 5 minutes. Drain them.

To make the stuffing, sauté the onion and the celery in the butter and proceed as for Stuffed Tomatoes.

STUFFED SUMMER SQUASH

1 medium summer squash

Parboil the squash in boiling salted water for 10 minutes. Let it drain.

Split the squash lengthwise, scoop out the pulp and chop it. Press out the excess liquid and sauté the pulp with the onion and the celery in the butter. Proceed as for Stuffed Tomatoes.

STUFFED ONIONS

2 large onions (omit chopped onion from Basic Filling ingredients)

Peel the onions and parboil them in boiling salted water for 15 to 20 minutes. Cut off pointed ends of the onions, scoop out the centers and chop them. Sauté the chopped onion with the celery in the butter and proceed as for Stuffed Tomatoes.

Guacamole Salad

1 clove garlic, halved
1 ripe avocado
1–2 tablespoons lime or lemon juice
Dash of hot-pepper sauce
2 teaspoons grated onion
Salt
Lettuce leaves
1 tomato, peeled and chopped
½ cucumber, peeled and chopped
1 green pepper, seeded and chopped

Rub the inside of a small bowl with the garlic halves and then discard them. Peel the avocado and mash the pulp with a fork in the same bowl. Add the lime juice, hot-pepper sauce and onion and mix. Season with salt to taste.

Arrange some lettuce leaves on a small platter and mound the avocado in the center. Heap the tomato, cucumber and green pepper around the edge. Chill until serving time.

Serve as an appetizer, accompanied by corn chips.

Antipasto Salad

This recipe, though it sounds complicated to shop for, is actually an excellent way for those who are cooking for two to use up scraps of this and that in the refrigerator. Be flexible in substituting.

VINAIGRETTE DRESSING

Combine:
  ½ cup olive or vegetable oil
  ¼ cup wine vinegar
  ½ teaspoon salt
  Freshly ground pepper
  1 small clove garlic, minced
  Pinch of dried oregano, crumbled
  Pinch of dried basil, crumbled

SALAD

¼ pound small mushrooms, washed and trimmed
1 small head romaine lettuce
1 or 2 slices each salami and ham, cut in strips
¼ pound provolone, cubed
1 4-ounce jar roasted red peppers, drained
1 2-ounce can anchovies, rinsed and drained
1 tablespoon capers
Black and green olives
1 hard-cooked egg, halved
1 tomato, peeled and cut in wedges

Put the mushrooms in a small saucepan, and pour ¼ cup of the dressing over them. Bring to a boil, cover and simmer over low heat for about 10 minutes. Set aside to cool.

Rinse 4 or 5 romaine leaves, break them into pieces and make a bed of them on a platter. Place the mushrooms in the center of the platter and group the remaining ingredients around them. Serve with salt, pepper and the vinaigrette dressing.

This is a substantial appetizer. It will take the place of a conventional salad when followed by a main-course pasta dish. It also makes a fine lunch, served with a loaf of Italian bread and followed by Italian ices.

Tomato Slices with Green Sauce

1 large beefsteak tomato or 2 medium tomatoes
¼ cup sour cream
3 tablespoons mayonnaise
2 tablespoons finely chopped parsley
1 green onion, finely chopped, including top
¼ cup finely chopped watercress, including stems
Lemon juice
Salt
White pepper

Cut the tomato in 6 thick slices and set aside. Combine in a bowl the sour cream, mayonnaise, parsley, green onion and watercress, and mix until well blended. Season to taste with lemon juice, salt and pepper.

Pour the sauce over the tomato slices and serve at room temperature.

Blue-Cheese Marinated Tomatoes

1 tablespoon red wine vinegar
2 tablespoons olive or vegetable oil
⅛ teaspoon salt
Pinch of white pepper
1 large beefsteak tomato or 2 medium tomatoes,
    in wedges
1–2 ounces blue cheese, coarsely shredded

Mix together the vinegar, oil, salt and pepper. Pour this
dressing over the tomato wedges and let them stand for
about ½ hour. Just before serving, sprinkle with shredded
blue cheese to taste. Serve at room temperature.

Tuna-Salad Mold

1½ teaspoons unflavored gelatin
1 can (7¾ ounces) tuna, drained
¾ cup finely diced celery
¼ cup finely diced green pepper
1 pimiento, chopped
Juice of ½ lemon
¼ cup of tomato juice
⅓ cup mayonnaise
½ teaspoon salt
Freshly ground pepper to taste
Salad greens
Pimiento cutouts
Parsley

Sprinkle the gelatin on 2 tablespoons of cold water in the top part of a small double boiler. Let it stand and soften, away from any heat, while you combine the other ingredients.

Mash the tuna well and mix in the celery, green pepper, pimiento, lemon juice, tomato juice, mayonnaise, salt and pepper. Dissolve the gelatin over hot water and stir it into the tuna mixture, combining it thoroughly.

Pack the mixture in a small oiled bowl that holds about 2 cups. Chill it for 3 hours or overnight. Dip the bottom of the bowl in hot water and unmold the salad onto a bed of greens. Garnish it with pimiento cutouts and sprigs of parsley.

Serve the salad for lunch with deviled eggs and sliced cucumbers.

Fish-Cucumber Salad

1 cup flaked cooked fish (about ½ pound fish fillets)
¼ cup peeled, finely chopped cucumber
¼ cup mayonnaise
1½ teaspoons lemon juice
Salt
Freshly ground pepper
Salad greens
1 hard-cooked egg, sliced
Green-pepper strips
Black olives
Tomato slices
Paprika

Combine the fish and the cucumber. Mix the mayonnaise with the lemon juice and add it to the fish mixture, tossing it all gently and taking care not to break up the fish. Season with salt and pepper to taste, and chill.

Shortly before serving, line a small shallow bowl with salad greens and heap the fish in the center. Garnish the edges with the sliced egg, green-pepper strips, black olives and tomato slices. Sprinkle the fish salad with a little paprika.

Serve this salad as an appetizer or double the recipe and serve it for lunch.

Sweet-Sour Bean Salad

1 can (9–11 ounces) small white beans
1 can (9–11 ounces) red kidney beans
2 green onions, thinly sliced
¼ cup finely diced green pepper
3 tablespoons salad oil
2 tablespoons vinegar
1 teaspoon sugar
¼ tablespoon salt
Dash of pepper

Put the white and red beans, the onion and the green pepper in a bowl. Mix the oil, vinegar, sugar, salt and pepper in a cup and pour over the vegetables, mixing gently. Chill for at least a few hours.

Serve as a side dish in place of a vegetable or salad.

Rice-Vegetable Salad

This recipe is nice from scratch, but is also a lovely way to use up leftover rice.

1 cup cooled cooked rice
⅓ cup coarsely shredded carrots
3 tablespoons diced celery
3 tablespoons diced green pepper
1 green onion, thinly sliced
1 pimiento, diced
2 tablespoons vegetable oil
1 tablespoon wine vinegar
Salt
Freshly ground pepper

Combine the rice, carrots, celery, green pepper, onion and pimiento. Mix the oil and vinegar, pour over the rice-and-vegetable mixture and toss it all well. Season to taste with salt and pepper. Chill.

This salad will keep well in the refrigerator for several days. Add some cold meat or chicken to it and it becomes a complete lunch.

Fresh-Corn Relish

3 ears of corn or ¾ cup canned, whole-kernel corn
½ small green pepper, chopped
½ cup celery, chopped
½ medium onion, chopped
1 teaspoon salt
½ teaspoon pepper
½ teaspoon dry mustard
Pinch of turmeric
2 tablespoons wine vinegar
¼ cup vegetable oil
1 pimiento, diced

If you use corn on the cob, cook the ears in boiling water for about 5 minutes. Cool them and cut the kernels from the cob. In a small bowl, combine the corn with the rest of the ingredients and mix well.

Refrigerate the relish for several hours before serving. It is especially good with ham or beef sandwiches.

Coleslaw

1½–2 cups coarsely shredded cabbage
½ small green or red pepper, cut in fine strips
1 tablespoon minced onion
¼ cup mayonnaise
2 tablespoons milk
1½ teaspoons cider vinegar
Salt
Freshly ground pepper

Combine the cabbage, pepper and onion in a mixing bowl and toss well. Put the mayonnaise, milk and vinegar in a small bowl or cup and beat them until they are smooth. Pour the mayonnaise mixture over the cabbage and vegetables and toss them again. Season the coleslaw to taste with salt and pepper. Refrigerate until ready to serve.

Green Salad

There is no "recipe" for a green salad; the ingredients will vary according to taste and the type of greens that are fresh and available at any particular time. Here are some general rules to follow:

Allow a good handful of salad greens per person. You will want two or more kinds of greens for an interesting salad, and even if you buy small quantities of each, there will be some left over. Do not wash the unused greens; store them in the refrigerator crisper for future use.

A large variety of lettuces and other greens is available the year round. Choose from the following: Belgian endive, bibb and Boston lettuce, Chinese cabbage, chickory, romaine lettuce, iceberg lettuce, dandelion greens, escarole, leaf lettuce, spinach leaves, fennel and watercress. For contrast, choose both light and dark leaves.

To prepare greens for salads, wash them thoroughly, changing the water frequently. The final water should be very cold. Shake the excess water from the greens and drain them well in a wire salad basket or in a clean, absorbent kitchen towel. If you are not using them right away, wrap the greens in a clean turkish towel or put them in a plastic bag or in a container with a tight-fitting lid. Then leave them in the refrigerator for a few hours to crisp.

Be sure that your salad bowl is large enough to hold the greens while you are tossing them. You may chill the bowl before filling it. To add more flavor to the salad rub the inside of the bowl with a split clove of garlic.

Tear the greens into bite-sized pieces and put them in the bowl with any other ingredients you wish to include. Add salad dressing just before serving and toss the salad lightly but thoroughly to coat each leaf.

Salad dressings serve three functions: they contribute to and bring out flavor, they bind the ingredients in the salad, and they add food value. Since much of a salad's taste and visual appeal lies in its crispness, do not use too much dressing, or the salad will be limp.

Four tablespoons (¼ of a cup) of salad dressing should be more than enough to toss a green salad for two. Three tablespoons of oil and 1 tablespoon of vinegar is a conventional proportion, but you may, of course, adjust the amount of vinegar according to your taste. Any favorite oil —olive, safflower, peanut, corn or vegetable—can be used.

Experiment with different kinds of vinegars—red-wine or white-wine, cider or herb—or use lemon or lime juice instead of vinegar. Add a pinch of chopped fresh or dried herbs such as thyme, tarragon, marjoram, basil, oregano or dill. A little dry or Dijon mustard, minced chives, garlic or parsley can also be added to the dressing.

Because the quantity of dressing required for two people is so small, we suggest that you make a half or even a full cup of your favorite dressing and keep it on hand in a jar in the refrigerator. Bring the dressing to room temperature and shake it well before using.

Chef's Salad

Like the Antipasto, this salad is a good way to stretch the odds and ends in your refrigerator into a satisfying dish for two.

VINAIGRETTE DRESSING

Combine:
  3 tablespoons salad oil
  1 tablespoon wine vinegar
  ¼ teaspoon prepared mustard
  Salt
  Freshly ground pepper

SALAD

2 cups salad greens, in bite-sized pieces
3 tablespoons chopped red onion
¼ cup slivered ham, tongue, turkey or chicken
¼ cup slivered Swiss cheese
¼ cup radish, cucumber or red onion slices
⅓ cup halved cherry tomatoes or tomato wedges
⅓ cup sliced cauliflorets or artichoke hearts
¼ cup pitted black olives
1 hard-cooked egg, quartered

Arrange the greens in a bowl and sprinkle them with the chopped red onion. Arrange the meat, cheese, vegetables, olives and egg in rows on the top of the greens.

Bring the bowl to the table, toss the salad with the dressing and serve with warm French bread for a spring or summer lunch.

SOUPS

Served with a green salad, crisp bread and dessert, full-bodied soups make a fine main course. Therefore most of these recipes yield about 4 cups of soup, enough for a generous main-course serving for two.

If you wish to serve soup *and* a main course, the recipes may provide more than you need. Remember, however, that most soups will keep in the refrigerator for at least a few days, and they usually taste even better when they are reheated. Many of them freeze well, too.

When freezer space is available, it makes sense to double or even triple these recipes. It's as economical and easy to make a lot of soup as a little. Since soup can be defrosted quickly, you will always have something on hand for a last-minute meal. To thaw, place the container of frozen soup in barely simmering water until the soup has liquefied enough to be transferred to a pot. Then just heat and serve.

Basic Soup Stock

This soup stock can be used in place of water or canned broth in many recipes. It is easy to make and adds immeasurably to the flavor of most soups. This recipe will produce about 4 quarts of stock, which you can freeze in pint or quart containers to have on hand when making soup.

About 3 pounds cracked beef or marrow bones
About 3 pounds beef shin or other soup meat
10 peppercorns
6 whole cloves
1 bay leaf
2 sprigs parsley
2 carrots
2 onions
2 ribs celery
1 tablespoon salt

Wash the bones and meat and put them in a large kettle or Dutch oven. Add 5 quarts of water and the rest of the ingredients. Bring the water to a boil, cover the pot and simmer for 3 hours, or until the meat is very tender. Remove the meat and strain the broth. Use the meat for sandwiches.

Pour the broth into four 1-quart containers and freeze immediately. Do not remove the fat that forms on top of the broth until you are ready to use the broth, because this excludes air and helps to preserve the stock. Do not let the stock cool down before freezing, or bacteria will grow.

Beef-Vegetable Borsch

This is a good way to turn small amounts of leftover beef or pot roast into a delicious, hearty meal for two.

2 tablespoons butter or margarine
1 small onion, chopped
1 carrot, sliced
½ small head cabbage (about ¾ pound), shredded
2 tablespoons tomato paste
2 cups beef stock or canned broth
2–2½ teaspoons vinegar
1 can (about 8 ounces) beets, in thin strips, undrained
½–1 cup diced cooked beef
Salt
Freshly ground pepper
Sour cream (optional)

Melt the butter in a medium saucepan and add the onion, carrot and cabbage. Sauté, stirring frequently, for about 5 minutes. Add the tomato paste, stock, 2 teaspoons of the vinegar, beets and meat. Bring it all to a boil, then lower the heat and simmer, covered, for 30 to 45 minutes or until the vegetables are very tender.

Season to taste with about 1 teaspoon of salt and freshly ground pepper. Adjust the vinegar flavor, adding more vinegar if necessary.

When you serve the borsch, top each bowl with a spoonful of sour cream, if you wish. Sprinkled with dill and accompanied by boiled potatoes and some crusty black bread, borsch makes a substantial main course.

Chickpea Soup with Pork

½ pound dried chickpeas
1 medium onion, chopped
¼ pound garlic-flavored sausage, sliced
¼ pound lean pork, in small cubes
2 tablespoons vegetable oil
Salt
1 package (10 ounces) frozen chopped spinach
1 hard-cooked egg, chopped

Cover the chickpeas with cold water and soak them overnight.

Drain the chickpeas after they have finished soaking. Sauté the onion, sausage and pork in the oil in a heavy kettle or Dutch oven until the meat is cooked through. Drain off the fat and deglaze the pan with about ½ cup water. Add the chickpeas, 1 teaspoon salt and 3½ cups of water. Bring the water to a boil, cover the pot and let the contents simmer for 2½ to 3 hours, or until the chickpeas are soft.

Add the frozen spinach and cook for 5 to 10 minutes more. Stir well, add more salt to taste and serve with a sprinkling of chopped egg on each bowl.

Lamb-Barley-Mushroom Soup

This soup should be made at least one day before you plan to serve it. It will keep well in the refrigerator and can also be frozen.

1 lamb shank, about 1½ pounds
Salt
¼ teaspoon peppercorns
Few sprigs parsley
1 large carrot, peeled, in 2″ pieces
1 small onion, studded with 2 whole cloves
⅓ cup medium pearl barley
¼ pound fresh mushrooms, trimmed and thinly sliced
Freshly ground pepper

Wipe the shank and trim off any excess fat. Put it in a kettle or Dutch oven with 1 quart of water, ½ teaspoon of salt, the peppercorns, parsley, carrot and onion. Bring the contents of the pot to a boil, cover the pot and simmer for 2 hours.

Remove the shank and let it cool. Strain the broth. Cut the meat off the shank in small pieces and add it and the carrot to the strained broth. Chill overnight.

The next day, lift off the solidified fat and discard it. Return the soup to the stove, and add the barley and mushrooms. Bring the soup to a boil and then simmer it, covered, for 1 hour, or until the barley is tender. Season the soup to taste with salt and pepper.

Corn Chowder

2 slices lean bacon
1 onion, chopped
¼ cup chopped celery, including leaves
½ bay leaf, crumbled
1 tablespoon flour
1½ cups diced peeled potatoes
1 can (8 ounces) cream-style corn
1 cup evaporated milk
Salt
Freshly ground pepper
Chopped parsley

Fry the bacon in a pot until it is crisp and brown. Remove it from the pot, crumble it and pour off all but 2 tablespoons of bacon fat. Cook the onion, celery and bay leaf in the hot bacon fat for about 5 minutes. Blend in the flour. Stir in 2 cups of water and the diced potato; bring to a boil and simmer, covered, for 15 minutes. Add the corn and the milk and heat well. Season to taste with salt and pepper.

Just before serving, add the crumbled bacon and garnish with chopped parsley.

Onion-Potato Soup

2–3 tablespoons butter or margarine
2 medium onions, thinly sliced
2 or 3 medium potatoes, peeled and thinly sliced
3 cups chicken broth
4 peppercorns
4 whole allspice
½ cup finely chopped celery tops
⅓ cup heavy cream
Salt
Freshly ground pepper

Melt the butter in a heavy kettle or Dutch oven. Add the onions and potatoes and sauté them, stirring, for about 5 minutes. Add the broth, peppercorns and allspice, bring it all to a boil and then simmer, covered, for about 30 minutes, or until the potatoes are tender. Beat the soup with a whisk until the potatoes are in small pieces.

Before serving, add the celery tops and the cream. Reheat the soup and season it to taste with salt and pepper.

If you keep this soup too long or freeze it, the potatoes may become too soggy.

Minestrone

1½ tablespoons olive or vegetable oil
⅓ cup diced celery
1 small onion, chopped
1 small clove garlic, minced
¾ cup shredded cabbage
3 cups beef stock or broth
1 can (8 ounces) tomatoes
Pinch of basil
Pinch of oregano
¼ cup broken-up vermicelli or fine noodles
¾ cup canned small white beans or chickpeas
Salt
Freshly ground pepper
Grated Parmesan cheese

Heat the oil in a kettle or Dutch oven. Add the celery, onion, garlic and cabbage and sauté them lightly for a few minutes. Add the stock, tomatoes, basil and oregano, and bring to a boil. Add the vermicelli, cover and simmer for about 15 minutes. Add the beans and simmer for 5 minutes more.

Season to taste with salt and pepper. Serve with grated cheese.

This soup will keep well in the refrigerator for a few days or more. It may also be frozen.

Fresh Tomato Soup

2 cups peeled and diced ripe tomatoes
¼ cup butter or margarine
2 tablespoons flour
1 teaspoon salt
Freshly ground pepper
Pinch of ground nutmeg
Pinch of basil
¼ teaspoon baking soda
1 cup light cream or half-and-half
½ cup dry white table wine

Simmer the tomatoes and butter in a saucepan for about 5 minutes. Purée them in a blender and return them to the pan. Blend in the flour, salt, pepper, nutmeg and basil, and bring the mixture to a boil, stirring constantly. Reduce the heat and simmer for about 2 minutes more, continuing to stir. Add the soda and the cream and cook over low heat, stirring, until slightly thickened. Stir in the wine and simmer for another few minutes before serving.

Sauerkraut Soup with Sausage

1 strip bacon, diced
1 small onion, finely chopped
¼ teaspoon paprika
1 can (7¾ ounces) sauerkraut, rinsed and drained
3 cups beef broth or stock
1 cup diced peeled potatoes
1 small bay leaf
½ pound kielbasa or other ready-to-eat spicy sausage
Salt
Freshly ground pepper
Chopped parsley

Put the bacon in a heavy kettle or Dutch oven. Cook it over low heat for a few minutes until some of the fat is rendered. Add the onion and sauté, stirring occasionally, for about 3 minutes. Add the paprika, sauerkraut, broth, potatoes and bay leaf. Bring the contents of the pot to a boil, cover and simmer for 35 minutes. Add the sausage and simmer for 15 minutes. Remove the sausage and let it cool until it can be handled. Discard the casing and cut the meat in ½-inch slices. Return the sausage to the soup, reheat and season it to taste with salt and pepper. Sprinkle with parsley before serving.

This soup will keep well in the refrigerator for several days.

Hearty Fish Soup

This recipe is a good way to stretch your leftover cooked fish into a delicious main course for two.

2 slices bacon, diced
⅓ cup chopped onion
⅓ cup chopped celery, including tops
⅓ cup thinly sliced carrot
2 cups fish broth or 1 cup canned chicken broth mixed
    with 1 bottle (8 ounces) clam juice
1 can (8 ounces) tomatoes
1 can (8¾ ounces) small white beans or kidney beans,
    drained
½–1 cup flaked cooked fish
Salt
Freshly ground pepper

Brown the bacon in a heavy kettle or Dutch oven. Add the onion, celery and carrot, and sauté them for 5 minutes. Cover and cook over low heat for 15 minutes. Add the broth, tomatoes and beans, and simmer it all for another 15 to 20 minutes. Add the fish and cook for 10 minutes more, seasoning to taste with salt and pepper.

Serve hot with biscuits or crackers.

New England Clam Chowder

12 chowder clams, or 1 can (6½ ounces) minced clams
1 stalk celery
2 small onions, diced
¼ pound salt pork or bacon, diced
2 small potatoes, peeled and diced
2 cups milk
Salt
Freshly ground pepper

If you are using fresh clams, scrub them and put them in a pot with the celery and 1 cup of water. Cover the pot and simmer the clams for about 15 minutes, or until the shells open. Strain the clam broth and set it aside. Cut up the clams and reserve them.

Cook the salt pork slowly in a heavy kettle until it is browned. Pour off all but 2 tablespoons of the fat, add the onions to the pork and cook them slowly until they are tender and transparent, but not browned. Add the potatoes and clam broth to the pot; bring the broth to a boil. Cover the pot and simmer it all for about 20 minutes, or until the potatoes are just tender. Add the clams and simmer for about 5 minutes more, until the clams are heated.

Scald the milk. Add it to the soup before serving, and season the chowder with salt and pepper to taste. Serve it hot with pilot crackers.

The potatoes in the chowder may become soggy if you keep it for too many days or freeze it.

Shrimp-Oyster Gumbo

1 medium onion, chopped
1 red or green pepper, diced
2–3 tablespoons butter or margarine
¼ cup flour
1 can (15½ ounces) cut okra and tomatoes, drained
1 teaspoon gumbo-filé seasoning (optional)
½ pound uncooked shrimp, peeled and cleaned
6 shucked oysters with liquid
Salt
Freshly ground pepper
Hot-pepper sauce
About ¾ cup hot cooked rice

Using a heavy kettle or a Dutch oven, cook the onion and
pepper in the butter for 2 or 3 minutes. Add the flour and
cook for a few minutes more, browning it lightly. Add 4
cups of water, the okra and tomatoes and the filé. Cover
the pot and simmer for 30 minutes. Add the shrimp and
oysters and simmer for 10 or 15 minutes more. Season
to taste with salt, pepper and hot-pepper sauce.

Serve with a spoonful of rice in the center of each bowl.

Cold Chicken-Chutney Soup

Since this soup will most likely be the introduction to a meal rather than its main course, the recipe is for 2 cups. It can, of course, be doubled if you wish to serve the soup as a main course.

1 can (13¾ ounces) chicken broth
½ teaspoon curry powder
1½ tablespoons chopped mango chutney
1 egg yolk
¼ cup heavy cream
½ teaspoon lemon juice
3 tablespoons finely diced peeled cucumber
Leftover diced chicken (optional)

Put the chicken broth, curry powder and chutney in a saucepan and bring them to a boil. Stir well and remove the pot from the heat. Beat the egg yolk with the cream. Beat in a tablespoon or two of the hot chicken broth, then gradually add the egg-cream mixture to the broth in the saucepan, beating it in with a whisk. Put the pot over low heat and stir the soup until it is smooth and slightly thickened. Do not let it boil. Add the lemon juice and chill the the soup thoroughly in the refrigerator.

Serve it cold, sprinkled with the cucumber and with diced cooked chicken, if you have some.

Cold Cucumber Soup

Delicious and refreshing, but not a soup you would serve in large portions. This recipe is for 2 cups.

1½ cups plain yogurt
2 tablespoons finely chopped walnuts
¾ cup diced peeled cucumber
½ small clove garlic, minced
Salt
White pepper
2 walnut halves

Beat the yogurt until it is smooth. Add the chopped walnuts, cucumber and garlic to the yogurt and mix them in well. Season the soup to taste with salt and white pepper. Chill it thoroughly.

Add a walnut half to each bowl just before serving.

Cold Pea Soup

This recipe is for 2 cups, since this soup will probably be served as an introduction to a meal rather than as a main course.

1 package (10 ounces) frozen peas
1 cup broth or stock
¼ teaspoon dried mint leaves
½ cup light cream
Salt
Freshly ground pepper
Sour cream or croutons

Cook the peas in a little water until they are tender. Put them in a blender with the stock and mint leaves and blend them until they are fairly smooth. Add the cream and whirl a few seconds longer. Season to taste with salt and pepper and put the soup in the refrigerator to chill.

When you serve the soup, top each bowl with a little sour cream or some croutons.

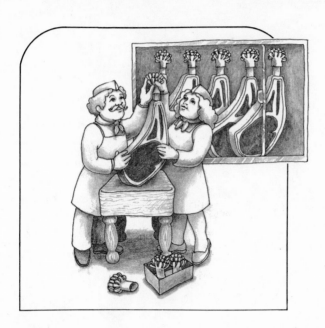

MEAT

MEAT AVAILABLE
IN SMALL QUANTITIES

There is no set rule concerning the amount of meat required to serve two people. Quantities will vary, depending on the type of meat you use and on the amount of other ingredients in the dish. However, here are some general guidelines to follow when buying meat for two people: allow ½ to ⅔ of a pound for lean, boneless meat, such as ground meat, stewing meat or boneless steak; allow 1 to 1½ pounds for meat with some bone, such as rib roast or unboned steak; allow 1½ to 2 pounds for very bony or fatty cuts, such as short ribs or brisket.

If you have a freezer, you can save time by cooking double quantities of certain recipes and freezing half for future use. There's hardly any extra effort involved in cooking four portions instead of two, and it is always a treat to have a fully prepared, home-cooked meal waiting in the freezer.

You can also save time—and money—if you plan ahead

and shop for several meals at a time. Buy meat on sale in larger quantities than you need and freeze the excess, or use it all in different kinds of dishes that won't seem repetitious. If you have freezer space available, you can buy a large piece of meat on sale and have the butcher cut it up for a number of different meals. A loin of pork, for example, will provide chops from the loin, a roast from the center and boneless stew meat from the other end. Package these in quantities for two and freeze them until you need them.

If you don't have freezer space, remember that ground meat should be used within twenty-four hours, chops and steaks will keep in the refrigerator for two or three days, and roasts will last a little longer.

Basic Hamburger Recipe

Some people prefer to shape unseasoned ground beef into patties and season them after they have been cooked. For those who prefer to season the meat before cooking, we offer the following basic recipe.

¾ pound ground beef
¼ cup minced onion
½ teaspoon salt
Freshly ground pepper
⅛–¼ cup tomato juice or ice water

Mix the ingredients lightly but thoroughly. Shape them into 2 thick patties. Broil, pan-fry or grill to desired doneness.

Serve plain, or on buns, or with one or a choice of several of the following hamburger toppings.

Hamburger Toppings

With the following toppings you can transform a simple hamburger into a zesty but inexpensive new dish. Be imaginative and substitute other vegetables and leftover ingredients you may have on hand. Each recipe makes enough topping for 2 large hamburgers, served with or without buns.

Pepper-Onion Topping

> 1 small onion, sliced lengthwise
> ½ small red pepper, in thin strips
> ½ small green pepper, in thin strips
> 2 teaspoons olive or vegetable oil
> Salt
> Freshly ground pepper

Sauté the onion and pepper slices in the oil, stirring frequently, until they are just tender. Season to taste with salt and pepper. Spread on cooked hamburgers just before serving.

Sauerkraut-Cheese Topping

> ½ can (4 ounces) sauerkraut
> ¼ teaspoon caraway seeds
> 2 slices Swiss cheese
> Chili sauce (optional)

Drain the sauerkraut well. Put it in a saucepan with 2 tablespoons of water and the caraway seeds. Cook for about 5 minutes, until the water has evaporated.

Top each cooked hamburger with sauerkraut and a slice of Swiss cheese. Put them in the oven or under the broiler until the cheese melts. Serve on buns, with chili sauce if you wish.

Cranberry-Celery Topping

> ⅓ cup cranberry sauce
> 2 tablespoons chopped celery
> ½ teaspoon minced onion
> Dash of lemon juice

Combine all of the ingredients thoroughly and spread on cooked hamburgers just before serving.

Blue-Cheese Topping

> 2 tablespoons crumbled blue cheese
> ⅓ cup sour cream
> 1 tablespoon finely sliced green onion

Mix the blue cheese with the sour cream and the green onion and spread on cooked hamburgers just before serving.

Italian-Style Topping

> 2 tablespoons tomato sauce
> Generous pinch of crushed oregano
> 2 slices muenster cheese

Simmer the tomato sauce with the oregano for a few minutes. Top each broiled hamburger with 1 tablespoon of the sauce and 1 slice of the cheese. Return them to the broiler until the cheese melts.

Stuffed Hamburgers

Shape ¾ pound of ground beef into 4 thin patties. Put the stuffing you have chosen on 2 of the patties. Using a spatula, place the remaining patties on top of the stuffed patties.

Press the edges together and broil or pan-fry, turning once, about 3 minutes on each side.

Stuffing #1

> **2 slices tomato**
> **2 tablespoons diced American cheese**
> **2 green onions, thinly sliced**
> **2 slices dill pickle**

Fill each set of patties with 1 slice of tomato, 1 tablespoon of cheese, 1 green onion and 1 slice of pickle. Cook and serve on toasted, buttered hamburger buns.

Stuffing #2

> **2 slices red onion**
> **2 slices green pepper**
> **1 tablespoon chili sauce**

Toss the onion and pepper slices in the chili sauce. Fill each set of patties with 1 slice of onion and 1 slice of pepper. Cook and serve on toasted English muffins.

Stuffing #3

> ½ cup cooked mashed potatoes
> 2 tablespoons chopped chives

Combine the potatoes with the chives. Divide the mixture in half and fill each set of hamburger patties. Cook and serve on toasted rye bread.

Savory Hamburgers

½–¾ pound ground beef
2 tablespoons sour cream
1 tablespoon bread crumbs
1 small can (4 ounces) mushroom stems and pieces, drained and chopped, or 6–8 fresh mushrooms, trimmed and chopped
1 green onion, finely sliced
1 tablespoon chopped parsley
½ teaspoon salt
Freshly ground pepper

Thoroughly mix all the ingredients and shape into 2 large patties. Broil, pan-fry or grill to the desired degree of doneness.

Individual Meat Loaves

¼ cup milk
¾ cup bread crumbs
¾ pound ground beef
1 teaspoon salt
Freshly ground pepper
1 egg, slightly beaten
3 tablespoons finely chopped celery
1 tablespoon minced onion
2 teaspoons chopped parsley
3 tablespoons chopped dill pickles

Preheat the oven to 375° F.

Add the milk to the crumbs. Mix the rest of the ingredients, then add the softened crumbs. Divide the mixture in half. Form each half into a small loaf and place the loaves on a lightly greased, shallow baking pan or in individual loaf pans. Bake for 30 to 40 minutes.

Eggplant and
Ground-Beef Casserole

Salt

1 eggplant (about ¾ pound), peeled and cut in ½-inch
  slices

Flour

1 egg beaten with 1 tablespoon milk

¼ cup bread crumbs

1 small clove garlic

About 3 tablespoons vegetable oil

½ pound ground beef

1 teaspoon salt

½ cup tomato purée or 2 tablespoons tomato paste mixed
  with enough water to make ½ cup

2 ounces (about ½ cup) mozzarella cheese, shredded

1 tablespoon chopped Italian or regular parsley

Freshly ground pepper

Salt the eggplant generously and let it stand for about 20
minutes. Stack it between paper towels and press out the
moisture. Coat the eggplant with flour, dip it in the beaten
egg and coat it again with bread crumbs.

Sauté the garlic in the oil until the garlic begins to
brown; discard it. Add the eggplant and brown it on both
sides, adding small amounts of additional oil if necessary.
Drain the eggplant on paper towels.

Preheat the oven to 375° F.

Using the pan in which you browned the eggplant,
brown the beef and drain off the fat. Add the teaspoon of
salt, tomato purée, cheese, parsley and pepper. Stir well.

Arrange eggplant slices and meat mixture in alternate layers in a small casserole, with some of the meat mixture on top. Bake for 45 minutes.

Squash with Beef-Rice Stuffing

1 acorn or butternut squash
½ pound ground beef
3 tablespoons chopped onion
¼ teaspoon salt
Freshly ground pepper
1 tablespoon tomato paste, mixed with enough water to
    make ¼ cup
Dash of Worcestershire sauce
Pinch of thyme
¾ cup cooked rice (¼ cup uncooked)

Preheat the oven to 350° F.

Wash the squash well, cut it in half and remove the seeds. Put it in a shallow baking dish, cut side down, and add about ½-inch of boiling water. Bake for 45 minutes, or until the squash is almost fork-tender.

While the squash is baking, brown the beef in a skillet. Add the onion and cook it until it is tender. Add the salt, pepper, tomato paste, Worcestershire sauce and thyme and simmer for a few minutes. Stir in the cooked rice.

Turn the squash so that the cut side is up and divide the meat-rice filling between the two halves. Shape the filling in mounds. Add more boiling water if necessary and return the pan to the oven. Bake for about 30 minutes more, until the squash is tender and the filling is well cooked.

Stuffed Cabbage Rolls

You will only need a few cabbage leaves to prepare this dish. Use the remaining cabbage to make Coleslaw (page 32) or Beef-Vegetable Borsch (page 41).

Four large cabbage leaves
6–8 ounces ground beef
½ medium onion, chopped
⅓ cup cooked rice
1½ tablespoons freshly grated Parmesan cheese
¼ teaspoon salt
Freshly ground pepper
1 tablespoon tomato paste mixed with enough water to
     make ¼ cup
¼ teaspoon chili powder

Blanch the cabbage leaves in boiling water for about 3 minutes. Run them under cold water and drain them well. Pat them dry and set them aside.

Mix together the beef, onion, rice, cheese, salt and pepper. Blend the tomato paste with the chili powder and add about 1 tablespoon of it to the meat mixture.

Preheat the oven to 350° F.

Divide the meat mixture evenly among the cabbage leaves, placing it near the base of each leaf. Fold the leaf base over the filling, then roll toward the tip of the leaf. Fold the outer edges of the leaf under.

Arrange the cabbage rolls in a small baking dish and spoon the remaining tomato sauce over them. Cover the pan with foil and bake for about 1 hour.

Barbecued Beef on Skewers

If you use a good grade of steak in this recipe, it will turn out better. Since you only need ½ pound for two people, it won't be too expensive even if you buy top-quality meat.

½ pound sirloin or other steak, in 1½-inch cubes
⅓ cup plain yogurt
¼ teaspoon ground ginger
½ small onion, minced
1 teaspoon ground coriander
½ teaspoon turmeric
½ teaspoon poppy seeds
Pinch of cayenne
½ teaspoon salt
1 large green pepper, in 1½-inch pieces
8 small whole mushrooms, washed and trimmed
1 large tomato, in wedges
2 tablespoons butter or margarine, melted

Put the meat in a bowl and cover it with boiling water. Let it stand for 5 minutes, then drain it.

Blend the yogurt, ginger, onion, coriander, turmeric, poppy seeds, cayenne and salt, then add to the meat, stirring well. Mix in the green pepper pieces and the mushrooms, and let everything stand at room temperature for 1 hour or more.

String the meat, green pepper, mushrooms and tomato wedges on small skewers. Baste with melted butter and put the skewers under a broiler or on a charcoal grill. Cook for 7 to 10 minutes, testing with a knife to see if the meat is done according to your preference. Turn the skewers once while cooking and baste everything again with the butter.

Serve this dish with plain rice or Rice Pilaf (page 195).

Teriyaki Steak

½–¾ pound boneless chuck-shoulder steak, about 1½ inches thick

2 tablespoons peanut oil

2 tablespoons soy sauce

1 tablespoon dry sherry

1 teaspoon minced fresh gingerroot or ½ teaspoon ground ginger

¼ teaspoon sugar

1 small clove garlic, minced

Trim the steak and place it in the freezer for about 20 minutes to make slicing easier.

In a mixing bowl, combine 1 tablespoon of the peanut oil with the rest of the ingredients. Set the bowl aside.

Using a very sharp knife, cut the steak across the grain at a slight angle in ⅛-inch slices. Put it in the bowl, stirring it well to coat the meat. Leave it at room temperature for 1 hour, stirring occasionally, or let it marinate overnight in the refrigerator.

Drain and reserve the marinade. Heat the remaining oil in a skillet. Add the meat and stir-fry for 3 or 4 minutes, until the meat loses its pink color. Heat the reserved marinade and pour on top of the meat before serving.

Flank Steak with Smothered Onions and Mushrooms

2 tablespoons butter or margarine
½ pound mushrooms, thinly sliced
2 large onions, thinly sliced
Salt
Freshly ground pepper
1 beef flank steak, about 1 pound or a little less
1 tablespoon vegetable oil
1 tablespoon Worcestershire sauce
Paprika

Melt the butter in a skillet. Add the mushrooms and onions and sauté, stirring occasionally, over low heat until the onions are golden. Season with salt and pepper to taste and set aside, keeping mixture warm.

Trim any excess fat from the steak. Using a sharp knife, score the meat about ⅛″ deep on both sides in a diamond pattern. Combine the oil and Worcestershire sauce with a liberal amount of freshly ground pepper and brush the mixture onto both sides of the steak. Sprinkle the steak lightly with paprika.

Broil the steak on a rack about 4 inches from the heat. Let it cook for about 4 minutes on each side for medium-rare.

Slice the steak across the grain in thin diagonal slices. Serve it with the mushroom-onion mixture and the pan juices.

Beef Burgundy

*This stew is even better when prepared a day or more
ahead. Since it takes a while to cook, it is a good dish to
prepare the night before or on the weekend for a week-
night meal that can be reheated quickly.*

1 slice bacon, in small pieces
½ pound chuck or other stew meat, in 1½-inch pieces
1 medium onion, chopped
1 small clove garlic, minced
1 carrot, sliced
1 tablespoon chopped parsley
4 peppercorns
Pinch of thyme
½ teaspoon salt
½–1 cup red Burgundy wine
3–4 ounces flat noodles

Cook the bacon over low heat in a medium skillet until
it gives off its fat and is slightly browned. Add the meat to
the pot and brown it over high heat, stirring frequently.
Add the onion, garlic and carrot, lower the heat and cook
until the onion is tender.

Add the parsley, peppercorns, thyme, salt and wine.
Bring it all to a boil, cover and simmer, adding more wine
if necessary, for 2 to 2½ hours, or until the meat is tender.

Serve the stew with hot buttered noodles.

Beef Stroganoff

If you can't find small quantities of chuck steak in your market, ask the butcher to cut part of a larger piece for you. Or buy a large quantity and use the excess to make Beef Burgundy (opposite) or Teriyaki Steak (page 69).

About ½ pound boneless chuck steak
2 tablespoons butter or margarine
1 onion, thinly sliced
About 12 mushrooms, washed, trimmed and sliced
1½ teaspoons flour ⎫
¼ teaspoon paprika ⎪
¼ teaspoon salt   ⎬ mixed together
Dash of cayenne   ⎪
Dash of pepper   ⎭
½ cup sour cream, thinned with ¼ cup milk
3–4 ounces flat noodles

Trim off any fat and cut the meat against the grain in very thin strips. Heat the butter in a skillet and add the meat and onion slices. Cook, stirring, over high heat to brown a bit. Add the mushrooms, and a little more butter if necessary, cover the skillet and cook over low heat for 15 to 20 minutes, or until the meat is tender.

Add the seasoned flour to the pan and stir to mix all ingredients. Add the sour cream and simmer, stirring, until the liquid is thickened and smooth. Add more salt and pepper if necessary.

Serve with hot, lightly buttered noodles.

Braised Pork Chops

2 large thick shoulder pork chops
1 large apple, peeled, cored and cut in chunks
1 medium onion, coarsely chopped
2 small ribs celery, coarsely chopped
½ teaspoon grated lemon rind
½ teaspoon lemon juice
½ teaspoon salt
½ teaspoon sage
Freshly ground pepper

Preheat the oven to 450° F.

Trim any excess fat from the chops. Put them in a small roasting pan and brown them in the oven for 15 minutes. Drain off any fat.

Combine the rest of the ingredients and spoon the mixture onto the chops. Cover the pan with foil, reduce the oven heat to 350° F. and roast the chops for about 50 minutes, or until they are tender.

Curried Pork

½ pound lean pork, diced
1 tablespoon butter or margarine
1 small onion, chopped
1 apple, peeled and diced
1 tablespoon flour
1 teaspoon curry powder
Pinch of ginger
Pinch of garlic powder
1 cup beef bouillon
2 teaspoons lemon juice
2 cups hot cooked rice

Brown the pork in the butter in a medium skillet. Add the
onion and apple and brown lightly, adding more butter
only if necessary. Stir in the flour, curry powder, ginger,
garlic powder, bouillon and lemon juice and bring to a
boil. Lower the heat and simmer, covered, for about 35
minutes. Serve on hot cooked rice.

Pork Chops with Paprika-Dill Sauce

3 tablespoons flour seasoned with salt and pepper to taste
2 large thick shoulder pork chops
2 tablespoons butter or margarine
1 large onion, thinly sliced
1 small clove garlic, minced
2 teaspoons paprika, or to taste
1 chicken bouillon cube dissolved in ½ cup boiling water
½ cup sour cream
1 teaspoon fresh or dried dill

Set aside 1 tablespoon of the seasoned flour and dredge the chops in the remaining 2 tablespoons of flour. Heat the butter in a skillet and brown the chops on both sides. Set the chops aside.

Add the onion and garlic to the skillet and sauté over medium heat, stirring occasionally, until the onion is tender. Stir in the paprika and the bouillon and cook over high heat, scraping to deglaze the pan. Add the chops, bring to a boil, reduce the heat, cover the pan and simmer for about 45 minutes, or until the chops are tender. Remove the chops to a serving platter and keep them warm.

Blend the reserved flour and the dill into the sour cream, then add it to the onion mixture remaining in the pan. Cook, stirring, over medium heat until the sauce thickens and is smooth; do not allow it to boil. Pour the sauce over the chops and serve them immediately.

Frankfurter-Potato Skillet

2 potatoes, peeled and thinly sliced
2–4 tablespoons butter or margarine
1 small onion, thinly sliced
¼ cup chopped green pepper
2 tablespoons chopped pimiento
½ cup chopped dill pickle
¼ teaspoon salt
Freshly ground pepper
¼ pound frankfurters, in 1-inch pieces

Cook the potatoes in a skillet in 2 tablespoons of the butter until they are browned on both sides. Add the rest of the ingredients. Cook over low heat, covered, adding more butter if necessary, until the potatoes are tender, for about 15 minutes.

English Sausages in Ale

½ pound link pork sausages
½ cup ale
1 bay leaf
3 peppercorns   } tied in a cheesecloth bag
3 whole cloves
Scrambled eggs, buttered toast, parsley (optional)

Put the sausages in an unheated heavy skillet. Cook them slowly in their own fat over low heat until they are nicely browned but not done. Pour off the fat. Add the ale and the bag of spices and simmer, covered, for about ½ hour, adding more ale if the skillet becomes dry.

Serve with scrambled eggs, buttered toast and a few sprigs of parsley as a brunch or light supper.

Armenian Shish Kebab

½ pound boneless lamb, in 1½-inch pieces
½ cup red wine
¼ teaspoon ground cumin
6 small white onions
1 large green pepper, in chunks
8–10 cherry tomatoes
¾ pound zucchini, in large chunks
8 whole mushrooms
Olive or vegetable oil

Marinate the lamb in the wine and cumin for at least 2 hours. Thread the lamb on a skewer, reserving the marinade.

To facilitate peeling, cover the onions with boiling water and let them stand for 5 minutes. Drain, peel and thread them on a separate skewer. Put each vegetable on a separate skewer, brush each with oil and set aside.

Grill the lamb under the broiler or over white-hot coals, turning occasionally and basting with the marinade until the lamb is cooked according to your preference. Test it by cutting into a piece with a sharp knife.

When the lamb is done, keep it warm while grilling the vegetables. The onions, peppers and zucchini will require more time than the tomatoes and the mushrooms.

You may use steak cubes if you wish, instead of lamb. Shish kebab is always good with rice.

Lamb Pilaf

This dish is an excellent way to stretch a very small amount of meat, only one chop, into a complete main dish for two.

1 shoulder lamb chop, about 7–8 ounces
1–2 tablespoons vegetable oil
¼ cup finely chopped onion
1 tablespoon pine nuts (optional)
½ cup uncooked rice
1 tablespoon raisins
About ½ teaspoon salt
Freshly ground pepper
Dash of sage
Dash of allspice
1 fresh or canned tomato, peeled and chopped
Chopped parsley

Remove the meat from the bone and cut it in small pieces. Brown the meat lightly in the oil. Remove it from the pan and set it aside.

Add the onion to the skillet and cook until it is tender but not brown. Add the nuts and the rice and cook them over medium heat, stirring constantly, for 5 minutes. Add 1 cup of water, the raisins, salt, pepper, sage, allspice and tomato. Bring the water to a boil, stir thoroughly, cover and cook over low heat, without stirring, for 20 to 30 minutes, or until the rice is tender and the liquid is absorbed.

Add the meat to the rice, stir it gently and let it heat through. Add more salt if necessary and let the pilaf stand for a few minutes before serving it. Serve it sprinkled with chopped parsley.

Chicken Livers with Bacon

2 slices bacon
½ pound chicken livers
1 small onion, thinly sliced
¼ pound mushrooms, thinly sliced
1–2 tablespoons sherry
1½ cups hot cooked rice
Chopped parsley

Cook the bacon in a skillet until it is crisp. Remove the bacon and set it aside in a warm place. Pour off and reserve all but 1 tablespoon of the bacon grease.

Wash the chicken livers and pat them dry. Sauté them in the hot bacon grease, allowing about 1 minute to each side. Remove the livers and set them aside with the bacon. Add the onions and mushrooms to the pan, adding a little more bacon grease if necessary, and sauté until lightly browned. Return the bacon and the livers to the pan, add a little of the sherry and reheat. Serve over hot cooked rice and garnish with chopped parsley.

Veal Rosemary

1 tablespoon cooking oil
1 tablespoon butter or margarine
½ pound boned veal shoulder, in 1-inch cubes
1 small onion, chopped
1 tablespoon flour
½ teaspoon crumbled rosemary leaves
1 cup (8-ounce can) tomatoes
¼ cup dry white wine
Salt
Freshly ground pepper
¼ pound mushrooms, trimmed and sliced

Heat the oil and butter in a skillet. Add the veal and onion and cook them, stirring from time to time, until they are browned. Stir in the flour and the rosemary. Add the tomatoes and wine. Bring it all to a boil, stirring constantly, and season to taste with salt and pepper.

Preheat the oven to 350° F.

Add the mushrooms and pour everything into a small casserole. Cover the casserole and bake for about 1 hour, or until the veal is tender, adding a little water or wine if necessary.

This dish is good with rice or mashed potatoes. It may be prepared ahead of time and reheated. It can also be frozen.

LARGE CUTS OF MEAT

Some of the best and most festive cuts of meat can *not* be purchased in quantities small enough to serve just two. Beef, pork and lamb roasts, baked or potted, produce much more than two servings, even if you buy small ones. The same is true of smoked and corned meats such as ham, corned beef and tongue. Very small pieces of pot roast or ham, when they *are* available, are often inferior in quality to larger ones.

Despite all this, there is no reason to exclude large roasts from your menus when you are cooking for two. This section provides basic recipes for cooking pot roast, boiled beef, pork roast, leg of lamb, ham, corned beef and then shows you how to use the leftovers in hot meals, salads and sandwiches. Since most of the basic recipes require a good deal of cooking time—roasts always do—we suggest that you prepare them on weekends or for guests and use the leftovers in quick meals during the week.

There are also recipes in other sections of this book for appetizers, soups, pasta and rice dishes which call for cooked meat, so keep this in mind when you have roast meat leftovers.

Many leftover meats freeze well. They can be packaged, preferably unsliced, and stored frozen if you have freezer space available. It is always useful to have cooked meats on hand.

POT ROAST WITH VEGETABLES (Basic Recipe)

This recipe will serve two, with enough meat left over to make a number of other meals.

About 4 or 5 pounds chuck or bottom round
1 tablespoon vegetable oil (if necessary)
Salt
Freshly ground pepper
¼ cup red wine
1 small onion, sliced
2 potatoes, peeled
4 carrots, peeled
1 medium zucchini, sliced
Flour (optional)

Brown the meat on all sides in a heavy kettle or Dutch oven, adding the oil if necessary. Season the meat with salt and pepper while browning it. Remove the meat from the pot.

Add the wine to the pot and scrape the bottom well. Put the onion and the meat in the pot, cover and simmer, turning the meat occasionally, for 2½ to 3 hours, or until the meat is just tender. Add more wine if necessary.

Add the potatoes and the carrots and simmer, covered, for another 30 minutes. Add the zucchini and simmer for 15 minutes more, or until everything is tender.

Remove the meat and the vegetables to a serving platter. You may thicken the gravy, if you wish, with a tablespoon or so of flour blended with a little cold water. Slice the meat fairly thin and serve it with the vegetables and the gravy.

Beef-Mushroom Burgundy

A simple but elegant dish to make with leftover pot roast.

¾ cup pot-roast gravy
About 1½ cups diced leftover pot roast
¼ pound fresh mushrooms, sliced
2 tablespoons red Burgundy wine
3–4 ounces flat noodles
Chopped parsley

Combine the gravy, meat, mushrooms and wine in a saucepan. Cook, covered, over medium heat for about 10 minutes.

Meanwhile, cook the noodles in boiling water. Drain and toss them lightly with butter. Pour the meat over the noodles and serve sprinkled with chopped parsley.

Beef Pasties

This recipe will make 8 pasties, using leftover pot roast. This is more than you will need for two people, but the extras can be frozen and served as an appetizer or as an accompaniment to soup. Or cut the recipe in half if you have less than a cup of leftover meat. The extra dough can be frozen and stored for future use.

⅓ cup leftover pot-roast gravy
1½ cups finely chopped leftover pot roast
1 tablespoon finely chopped onion
Butter or margarine
1 teaspoon prepared mustard
Salt
Freshly ground pepper
1 package piecrust mix for 2-crust pie, or your own
   favorite pie dough

Mix the gravy and the meat. Sauté the onion in a little butter until it is tender, then add it to the beef with the mustard and a generous dash of salt and pepper.

Preheat the oven to 450° F.

Prepare the piecrust dough and roll it out to form two 10-inch squares. Cut each into four squares. Divide the meat mixture in four and put one heaping on each square. Wet the edges, fold the squares to form triangles and seal the edges with a fork.

Bake on an ungreased baking sheet for about 15 or 20 minutes, until the pasties are heated through and golden brown.

If you store them in the refrigerator, reheat them in a slow oven before serving.

Chili Beef Skillet

1 small onion, sliced
¼ cup chopped celery
1–2 tablespoons vegetable oil
About ¾ cup diced leftover pot roast
¾ teaspoon chili powder
2 tablespoons tomato paste, mixed with enough water to make ½ cup
1 can (about 8 ounces) whole-kernel corn, drained
1 can (about 8 ounces) red kidney beans, drained
¼ cup sliced pitted black olives
Salt
Freshly ground pepper
Corn chips

Cook the onion and the celery in the oil until they are crisp-tender. Add the meat and the chili powder and stir for a few minutes. Add the tomato paste, corn, beans and olives. Simmer, stirring occasionally, for about 10 minutes, seasoning to taste with salt and pepper.

Serve with corn chips.

Barbecued Beef and Beans

1 can (about 8 ounces) baked beans
1 can (about 8 ounces) lima beans, drained
¼ cup catsup
2 teaspoons vinegar
2 teaspoons brown sugar
¼ teaspoon dry mustard
About ¾ cup leftover pot roast, in chunks
1 small onion, chopped

Preheat the oven to 375° F.

Combine all the beans in a small casserole. Mix the catsup, vinegar, brown sugar and mustard together and stir about half of it into the beans. Top with the meat and onion and pour the remaining sauce over all.

Cover and bake for about 30 minutes, or until it is very hot.

Pot-Roast Sandwiches

Leftover pot roast makes a delicious filling for sandwiches, hot or cold.

Reheat the sliced meat in gravy and serve it on slices of white, whole-wheat or pumpernickel bread as open-faced sandwiches.

Or serve cold sliced beef with prepared mustard, mayonnaise, sliced onion and tomatoes on rye or crisp French bread.

BOILED BEEF WITH
VEGETABLES (Basic Recipe)

This recipe will serve two with plenty left over for Beef Salad and sandwiches. In fact, we have added 2 extra potatoes, which can be reserved for the Beef Salad recipe (page 91).

3–4 pounds beef brisket or boneless chuck
Salt
Pepper
Rosemary
1 rib celery, sliced
2 carrots, peeled and diced
1 leek, sliced (optional)
1 medium onion, halved
2 whole cloves
6 medium peeled potatoes
8 carrots
4 cabbage wedges
Mustard Sauce or Horseradish Sauce

Season the meat with salt, pepper and a little rosemary. Put it in a Dutch oven with the celery, carrots, leek, onion, cloves, 1 teaspoon of salt and enough water to cover the meat. Bring the water to a boil, cover the pot and simmer (do not boil) for 2 hours, or until the meat is almost tender.

Skim any fat from the broth and add the potatoes and carrots. Cook for 35 minutes, then add the cabbage and cook for 10 minutes longer, or until everything is tender. Do not overcook the cabbage.

Remove the meat and vegetables and serve the broth first.

Slice the meat thin and serve it on a platter with the vegetables and Mustard Sauce or Horseradish Sauce.

This dish can be prepared ahead and reheated. If the broth is refrigerated, fat will solidify on top of it. Remove this layer of fat before heating.

MUSTARD SAUCE

Combine:

> ½ cup sour cream
> 1 tablespoon prepared mustard
> 1 tablespoon minced onion
> ¼ teaspoon salt

HORSERADISH SAUCE

Combine:

> ½ cup sour cream
> 1½ tablespoons prepared horseradish
> ⅛ teaspoon salt

Beef Salad

Make this with leftover boiled beef and potatoes.

VINAIGRETTE DRESSING

Combine:
> ½ cup olive or vegetable oil
> 3 tablespoons wine vinegar
> Pinch of dry mustard
> Salt
> Freshly ground pepper

SALAD

2 cooked potatoes
Thin slices leftover boiled beef, enough for two persons
Broken salad greens
1 large tomato, in wedges
1 teaspoon capers
1 small red onion, thinly sliced

Put all the salad ingredients in a bowl and toss them with the dressing.

Boiled-Beef Sandwiches

Using good fresh bread, make sandwiches with thinly sliced beef, lettuce and leftover Mustard or Horseradish Sauce.

ROAST PORK SHOULDER
(Basic Recipe)

5-pound pork shoulder
Salt
Freshly ground pepper
1 clove garlic, cut
Sage (optional)
Flour

Preheat the oven to 325° F.

Put the meat, fat side up, on a rack in a shallow roasting pan. Rub it with salt, pepper, garlic and a little sage, if you wish. Insert a meat thermometer into the roast so that the tip is in the center but not touching any fat or bone.

Roast in the oven, uncovered, without adding any liquid, for about 3½ hours, or until the meat thermometer registers 185° F. Let the roast stand in the pot for about 15 minutes, then put the meat on a hot platter and make gravy by thickening the drippings with a little flour.

Roast pork is delicious served with braised cabbage, applesauce and roast potatoes.

Variations:

If you wish, you may marinate the pork roast for 2 to 4 hours at room temperature, or overnight in the refrigerator. Use one of the following marinades:

HERB MARINADE

Combine:

½ cup dry white wine
½ cup oil
¼ cup vinegar
1 teaspoon salt
1 teaspoon oregano
1 teaspoon basil
½ teaspoon pepper
2 cloves garlic, minced

SHERRY-SOY MARINADE

Combine:

½ cup dry sherry
⅓ cup soy sauce
1 clove garlic, minced
1 tablespoon dry mustard
1 teaspoon ground ginger
1 teaspoon sage or thyme

Sweet-Sour Pork

1 small onion, sliced lengthwise
½ cup thinly sliced carrots
½ large green pepper, in strips
1 tablespoon vegetable oil
About 1 cup leftover pork, in chunks
1 can (about 8 ounces) pineapple chunks, drained
2 teaspoons cornstarch
½ cup chicken broth
2 tablespoons cider vinegar
2 tablespoons brown sugar
1½ cups cooked rice

Sauté the onions, carrots and green pepper in the oil, stirring, for about 3 minutes, or until crisp-tender. Remove them from the pan. Brown the pork pieces in the pan and pour off any fat. Return the vegetables to the pan and add the drained pineapple.

Combine the cornstarch, broth, vinegar and brown sugar in a small saucepan. Bring the mixture to a boil, stirring, and let it simmer for a few minutes. Pour the sauce over the vegetables, meat and pineapple, and reheat it all together. Serve it hot, with rice.

Barbecued Pork on Buns

2 tablespoons chopped green pepper
1 tablespoon chopped onion
1 tablespoon vegetable oil
¾ cup diced leftover pork
¼ cup catsup
1 teaspoon prepared mustard
1 tablespoon brown sugar
1 teaspoon Worcestershire sauce
¼ teaspoon salt
2–3 sandwich buns

Sauté the green pepper and onion in the oil for about 2 minutes. Add the pork, catsup, mustard, brown sugar, Worcestershire sauce, salt and 2 tablespoons of water. Cook it all over low heat, stirring occasionally, for 15 minutes, or until it is thick.

Serve hot on toasted buns.

Roast Pork Sandwiches

Pork is especially good served cold, and leftover roast pork makes a fine sandwich filling.

Serve cold pork slices on rye bread with mustard and mayonnaise, or on pumpernickel with Swiss cheese, tomatoes and mustard. Or serve it on toasted buns topped with coleslaw seasoned with curry powder.

ROAST LEG OF LAMB (Basic Recipe)

1 whole leg of lamb, about 7 pounds
Salt
Freshly ground pepper
Rosemary

Preheat the oven to 325° F.

Season the meat with salt, pepper and rosemary. Place it, fat side up, on a rack in an open roasting pan. Insert a meat thermometer in the center, being careful not to have the tip touch the bone. Do not add water to the pan or cover it, and do not baste the meat while it is roasting.

Despite what it says on your meat thermometer, a leg of lamb will be well-done when the thermometer registers 165° F. In other words, allow about 15 minutes per pound for well done, 12 minutes per pound for medium-rare.

Allow the meat to "rest" for about 15 minutes before carving it.

Variations:

For variety, try brushing the lamb roast with one of the following glazes during the last hour or so of roasting:

GARLIC GLAZE

Combine:
- ⅓ cup dry sherry
- ⅓ cup water
- 1 tablespoon paprika
- ½ teaspoon basil
- 2 tablespoons soy sauce
- 2 tablespoons oil
- 3 cloves garlic, minced

JELLY GLAZE

Melt ¾ cup mint, currant or apricot jelly over low heat and brush on lamb.

SPICY GLAZE

Combine:
- ¼ cup firmly packed brown sugar
- 1 clove garlic, minced
- 1½ teaspoons salt
- ½ teaspoon dry mustard
- ½ teaspoon chili powder
- ¼ teaspoon ground ginger
- ¼ teaspoon ground cloves
- 1 tablespoon lemon juice

Lamb Curry

⅓ cup chopped onion
2 teaspoons curry powder
¼ teaspoon ground ginger
2 tablespoons vegetable oil
1 tart apple, peeled and chopped
1 cup chicken broth
1 tablespoon tomato paste
About 1 cup diced leftover lamb
1 tablespoon heavy cream
Salt
1½ cups hot cooked rice

Sauté the onion, curry powder and ginger in the oil, stirring, for about 3 minutes. Add the apple, broth and tomato paste. Bring to a boil; cover and simmer for about 20 minutes, or until the sauce is quite thick. Add the meat and simmer for about 10 minutes longer.

Before serving, add the cream and reheat, seasoning to taste with salt and more curry powder, if you wish. Serve the lamb over the rice with chutney, coconut, raisins, sliced banana and nuts as condiments.

Lamb and Vegetables

1 small onion, chopped
1 tablespoon vegetable oil
1 small clove garlic, minced
About 1 cup leftover lamb, in chunks
1 medium zucchini, in 1-inch slices
1 medium yellow squash, in 1½-inch chunks
1 potato, peeled and diced
2 tablespoons tomato paste mixed with enough water
   to make ½ cup
Salt
Freshly ground pepper

Sauté the onion in the oil until it is tender but not brown.
Add the garlic and sauté for 1 minute longer. Add the meat
and stir it in well. Add the zucchini, squash, potato, tomato paste and about ¼ cup of water. Season with salt
and pepper and mix well. Bring it to a boil, cover and simmer for about 30 minutes, adding more water if necessary, until the vegetables are tender and the mixture is
quite thick.

This dish may be prepared ahead and reheated.

BAKED HAM (Basic Recipe)

Buy a whole ham if you're having a lot of guests, or a half shank or butt if it's just for two.

1 half or whole ham, fully cooked
Cloves
Light-brown sugar

Preheat the oven to 325° F.

Put the ham on a rack and bake until it is heated through, allowing 10 to 15 minutes per pound. Remove the ham from the oven when it is heated, cut off any skin and some of the fat, if necessary. Score the top diagonally, insert the cloves in a diamond pattern and sprinkle the fat with a little light-brown sugar.

Increase the oven heat to 400° F. and bake the ham for about 15 minutes longer, or until it is lightly browned. Let the ham cool a bit before carving it.

Variations:

For variety, try glazing the ham with one of the following glazes (instead of the brown sugar) during the last 15 minutes of baking:

MOLASSES GLAZE

Mix ½ cup vinegar with ½ cup molasses.

JELLY GLAZE

Mash 1 cup cranberry, currant or other tart jelly.

Marmalade Glaze

Use ½ cup orange, peach or apricot marmalade.

Pineapple Glaze

Mix ½ cup crushed pineapple and ¾ cup packed brown sugar.

Honey Glaze

Use ¾ cup honey.

Honey and Peanut-Butter Glaze

Mix ½ cup honey and ½ cup smooth peanut butter.

Mustard-Molasses Glaze

Mix ½ cup sugar, ⅓ cup molasses and ½ teaspoon dry mustard.

Applesauce Glaze

Mix ½ cup corn syrup, 1 cup applesauce and 2 tablespoons prepared mustard.

Ham and Split-Pea Soup

You can serve this rich, flavorful soup as a main course.

1 leftover ham bone
½ pound green or yellow split peas, washed and drained
1 carrot, sliced
1 small onion, sliced
1 rib celery, sliced
Salt
Freshly ground pepper
1 cup diced leftover ham (or more, if you wish)

Put the ham bone, peas, carrot, onion, celery, ½ teaspoon of salt, some pepper and 1 quart of warm water in a heavy kettle. Let it all stand for about 1 hour.

Bring the water to a boil, cover the pot and simmer, stirring occasionally, for 1 hour, or until fairly thick. Remove the bone and cut off any meat. Put the meat back in the soup together with the diced ham and reheat, adding salt to taste.

Ham-Apple Slaw

1 cup shredded cabbage
About ½ cup slivered leftover ham
1 apple, peeled, cored and cut in pieces
2 tablespoons mayonnaise
½–1 tablespoon vinegar

Chill the cabbage and the ham. Just before serving, add the apple and stir in the mayonnaise and vinegar.

Baked-Ham Sandwiches

Sliced ham on rye bread with mustard and slices of Swiss cheese, Bermuda onion and tomato is always a favorite. You can also make ham-salad sandwiches, using diced ham and celery, a little minced onion, sweet pickle and enough mayonnaise to moisten the mixture. Try serving the ham salad on hard rolls with lettuce.

NEW ENGLAND CORNED-BEEF DINNER (Basic Recipe)

Increase the number of vegetables in this recipe according to the number of people you are serving. If you are cooking this dinner for two and expect to have lots of corned beef left over, cook some extra potatoes and reserve some of the broth to use for Corned-Beef and Potato Bake (below).

5 pounds corned-beef brisket
Peeled potatoes, 1 per serving
Peeled carrots, 1 or 2 per serving
Peeled small white turnips, 1 per serving
½ small head of cabbage, in wedges
Vinegar
Prepared mustard

Wash the beef and put it in a large kettle or Dutch oven. Cover it with cold water and bring to a boil. Cover the pot and simmer for 3 hours, or until the meat is tender. Remove the meat and skim off any excess fat from the liquid. Keep the meat warm.

Add the potatoes, carrots and turnips to the liquid in the kettle. Cover and simmer for 20 minutes, or until the vegetables are tender. Add cabbage and simmer for about 10 minutes more.

Slice the meat thin and arrange it on a platter with the vegetables. Serve with vinegar and mustard.

Corned-Beef and Potato Bake

1–2 tablespoons butter or margarine
1 small onion, chopped
1 small green pepper, in thin 1-inch-long strips
1½ teaspoons Worcestershire sauce
Pinch of dry mustard
¾ cup chopped leftover corned beef
1 cup chopped cooked potatoes
Leftover corned-beef broth

Melt the butter in a skillet, add the onion and green pepper and cook for a few minutes, until the vegetables are tender. Add the Worcestershire sauce, mustard, corned beef and potatoes. Mix well, adding a few tablespoons of corned-beef broth, enough to moisten the mixture.

Preheat the oven to 425° F.

Put the corned-beef mixture in a small, shallow baking dish. Bake it for 20 minutes, or until it is hot and lightly browned.

Corned-Beef Omelet

2 tablespoons butter or margarine
½ cup chopped leftover corned beef
1 green onion, sliced
4 eggs, lightly beaten with 2 tablespoons milk
Freshly ground pepper

Melt the butter in a 7- or 8-inch skillet. Add the corned beef and green onion, and sauté for a few minutes. Season the beaten eggs with some pepper. Pour them into the skillet over the meat and onions and cook fairly quickly, pulling the cooked eggs toward the center until they are lightly browned along the edges and on the bottom. Slide the omelet onto a platter and fold it.

Serve it at once with a tossed green salad.

Corned-Beef Sandwiches

Use leftover corned beef to make the following sandwiches:

GRILLED CORNED-BEEF SANDWICHES

Soak a few caraway seeds in hot water for a few minutes, then toss them with some drained sauerkraut. Spread 2 slices of rye bread with mayonnaise. Top each bread slice with thin slices of corned beef, some sauerkraut, a slice of Swiss cheese and another slice of rye bread. Brush both sides of the sandwiches with melted butter or margarine and grill them slowly on a grill or in a skillet, covering them from time to time if necessary, until they are lightly browned and the cheese has melted.

CORNED-BEEF SALAD SANDWICHES

Mix ½ cup of chopped cooked corned beef with ¼ cup of finely chopped celery, 1 tablespoon of minced onion, ¼ cup of mayonnaise and 1 tablespoon of prepared mustard. Spread on buttered rye bread to make 2 sandwiches.

SLICED CORNED-BEEF SANDWICHES

Combine thinly sliced corned beef with sliced American cheese, sliced dill pickle, lettuce and mustard. Or combine sliced corned beef with pickled beets, pickled cucumbers and a little horseradish. Serve as open-faced rye-bread sandwiches.

POULTRY

A good repertoire of poultry dishes is especially important to those who are cooking for two because poultry is available in small quantities and it is inexpensive. A small duck will serve two nicely, as will two Rock Cornish hens; and chicken, of course, is available in parts. When you buy chicken parts, you also have the advantage of being able to select exactly the type of meat that you prefer.

Poultry dishes are popular and usually very easy to prepare. Many of them are also quite elegant, and some of the recipes in this section provide simple, sophisticated food for candlelit dinners for two.

The quantities we suggest vary a bit, according to the amount of other ingredients in a dish. In general, allow about half of a 3- to 4-pound chicken, two whole chicken breasts or 1 to 1½ cups of diced, cooked meat.

Turkey is also available in parts, but even the parts provide too much meat for two. We suggest roasting a small whole turkey, then using the leftovers in a number of attractive ways.

Tarragon Chicken
and Vegetables

½ broiler-fryer (about 1½–2 pounds), in serving pieces
Salt
Freshly ground pepper
½ teaspoon dried tarragon or 1 teaspoon fresh
2 tablespoons chopped onion
2 medium potatoes, peeled and cubed
2 carrots, in ¼-inch slices

Preheat the oven to 400° F.

Wash the chicken and pat it dry with paper towels. Season it on all sides with salt, pepper and tarragon. Put the chicken in a Dutch oven, cover the pot tightly and bake the chicken for 30 minutes.

Push the chicken to one side of the casserole and add the vegetables on the other side. Season them with salt and pepper and stir them into the pan juices. Spread the vegetables out evenly and arrange the chicken over them. Cover the pot, return it to the oven and bake for 30 minutes more, or until the chicken and the potatoes are tender.

Baked Chicken
with Hot Mustard Sauce

½ broiler-fryer (about 1½–2 pounds), in serving pieces

⅓ cup evaporated milk   ⎤
                        ⎬ mixed together
1 tablespoon soy sauce ⎦

¾ cup cornflake crumbs   ⎤
¾ teaspoon salt   ⎬ mixed together
Dash of freshly ground pepper ⎦

Preheat the oven to 350° F. Grease a small shallow baking pan.

Dip the chicken pieces in the milk mixture, then roll them in the crumbs. Put them in the baking pan and bake them for 1 hour, or until the chicken is tender.

HOT MUSTARD SAUCE

2 tablespoons prepared mustard
½ teaspoon sugar
¼ teaspoon salt
Dash of hot-pepper sauce
¼ cup evaporated milk
½ teaspoon lemon juice

Just before the chicken is ready, prepare the Hot Mustard Sauce by mixing the mustard, sugar, salt, pepper sauce and milk in a small saucepan. Heat it all, stirring, then add the lemon juice.

Serve the chicken with the sauce on the side.

Middle Eastern Chicken with Bulgur

Bulgur is cracked buckwheat groats. It is available in stores that sell Middle Eastern food, in health-food stores, specialty stores and in some supermarkets.

1 tablespoon butter or margarine
1 tablespoon vegetable oil
½ broiler-fryer (about 1½–2 pounds), in serving pieces
Salt
Freshly ground pepper
1 medium onion, chopped
1 small clove garlic, minced
½ cup bulgur
Pinch of cardamom
Pinch of coriander
Pinch of ground cumin
1½ tablespoons lemon juice
1 cup boiling chicken broth

Heat the butter and oil in a skillet and brown the chicken in it, seasoning it with salt and pepper as it browns. Remove the chicken from the pan and cook the onion and garlic in the remaining fat until they are translucent. Add the bulgur, stirring it well to glaze it. Mix in the cardamom, coriander, cumin and lemon juice.

Preheat the oven to 350° F. Put the chicken in a casserole, cover it with the bulgur mixture and pour the broth over all. Cover the pot and bake for 1 hour, or until the chicken is tender.

Italian Chicken with Eggplant

2 tablespoons butter or margarine
½ broiler-fryer (about 1½–2 pounds), in serving pieces
Salt
Freshly ground pepper
1 small eggplant
Flour
Vegetable oil
1 small onion, chopped
1 clove garlic, minced
1 chicken bouillon cube
¼ cup dry red wine
2 tablespoons sliced stuffed green olives
1 pimiento, in strips

Melt the butter in a heavy skillet. Fry the chicken in the butter until it is golden brown on all sides. Season the chicken with salt and pepper, cover the skillet and cook the chicken over low heat, adding a little butter if necessary, for about 45 minutes or until it is tender.

Peel the eggplant and cut it in slices about ½-inch thick. Season them with salt, dip them in flour and brown them in oil until they are tender.

When the chicken is tender, remove it to a shallow baking dish. Preheat the oven to 400° F. Using the drippings in the pan in which the chicken was cooked, sauté the onion and the garlic for about 5 minutes. Stir in 1 tablespoon of flour, ½ cup of water, the bouillon cube and the wine. Bring it all to a boil and cook until it has thick-

ened, stirring from time to time. Pour the sauce over the
the chicken in the baking pan. Cover with the fried eggplant and sprinkle with the olives and pimientos. Bake for
about 25 minutes, or until everything is thoroughly heated.

Lemon Broiled Chicken

½ broiler-fryer (1½–2 pounds), in serving pieces
¼ cup fresh lemon juice
2 tablespoons vegetable oil
¼ teaspoon thyme
¼ teaspoon marjoram
½ teaspoon salt
1 teaspoon grated lemon rind

Preheat the broiler. Arrange the chicken pieces in a broiler
pan.

Combine the rest of the ingredients and brush the mixture on the chicken. Broil, about 6 inches from the heat, for
½ hour on each side, basting frequently with the lemon-
juice mixture.

Chicken Breasts and Mushrooms in Wine

1–2 tablespoons butter or margarine
2 whole chicken breasts, split
2 green onions, chopped
Salt
Freshly ground pepper
¼ pound sliced or small whole mushrooms, washed and
  trimmed
⅓ cup dry vermouth or white wine

Melt the butter in a skillet and brown the skin side of the
chicken. Turn the chicken over, add the onions and sauté
for 5 to 10 minutes or until the chicken is golden and the
onions are tender. Season to taste with salt and pepper.
Add the mushrooms to the pan, pour in the vermouth,
scraping any bits that are stuck on the bottom of the skillet, cover the pot and cook over low heat for 20 minutes,
or until the chicken is tender.

Remove the chicken, onions and mushrooms to a warm
platter. Cook the pan juices over high heat, stirring, for a
few minutes. Pour them over the chicken and serve it at
once.

Chicken Breasts
with Cheese Sauce

2 whole chicken breasts, split
2 slices bacon, cut in half
2 tablespoons butter or margarine
2 tablespoons flour
½ teaspoon salt
Freshly ground pepper
1½ cups milk or cream
⅓ cup grated Parmesan cheese (freshly grated if
   possible)

Preheat the oven to 400° F.

Arrange the chicken, skin side up, in a broiler-proof dish. Top each piece of chicken with a slice of bacon and bake the chicken for 25 minutes or until the bacon is crisp and the chicken is cooked through. Spoon off the fat.

While the chicken is baking, melt the butter in a small saucepan and add the flour, salt and pepper. Cook for a minute or two, stirring all the while, until the mixture is smooth. Gradually add the milk and cook, stirring, until the sauce thickens. Stir in the Parmesan cheese.

Spoon the sauce over the cooked chicken. Put it under the broiler for a few minutes until it is lightly browned. Serve at once.

Chicken Skillet Dinner

1 or 1½ whole chicken breasts, skinned and boned
2 tablespoons soy sauce
1–2 tablespoons oil
1 small onion, chopped
¼ pound mushrooms, washed, trimmed and sliced
½ cup uncooked rice
½ teaspoon celery seed
1½ cups chicken broth
⅓ cup frozen peas
Salt
Freshly ground pepper

not great

chicken was dry

Using a sharp knife, cut the chicken crosswise in ¾-inch strips. Put the chicken strips in a small bowl with the soy sauce and marinate them for about ½ hour.

Heat the oil in a medium skillet and stir-fry the chicken for about 2 minutes. Add the onion, mushrooms, rice and celery seed and stir-fry for a few minutes more. Add the broth and bring it to a boil. Reduce the heat, cover the skillet and simmer for about 12 minutes, without stirring. Add the peas and simmer for 3 minutes more or until the liquid is absorbed and the rice is cooked. Season to taste with salt and pepper.

Chicken Kiev

This classic dish is very simple to prepare. It requires last-minute cooking, which makes it a bit of a bother to fix for a large group, but perfect for a candlelit dinner for two.

½ stick butter (2 ounces)
2 whole chicken breasts, skinned, boned and halved
Fine dry bread crumbs
1 egg, beaten with 2 teaspoons cold water
Vegetable oil for deep-frying

Cut the butter in half lengthwise; then cut each piece in half lengthwise again to make four 2-inch pieces. Chill them in the refrigerator or freezer until they are very firm.

Pound the chicken, between two layers of waxed paper, into thin cutlets. Put a piece of butter in the center of each cutlet. Roll the chicken lengthwise around the butter, folding it tightly so that the butter will not escape during cooking. Secure the cutlets with toothpicks.

Roll the breasts in the bread crumbs, dip them in the beaten egg, then roll them in the bread crumbs again. Fry them in hot deep fat (375° F. on a frying thermometer) for 3 to 5 minutes, or until they are golden brown. Drain them and put them on a cookie sheet in a hot oven (425° F.) for 5 minutes before serving.

Sautéed Chicken Cutlets

2 whole chicken breasts, skinned and boned
Salt
Pepper
½ cup finely ground fresh bread crumbs
½ cup freshly grated Parmesan cheese
2 eggs, beaten
3 tablespoons butter or margarine

Put the chicken breasts between two layers of waxed paper and pound them to less than ¼-inch thickness. Cut each half in two crosswise. Season both sides lightly with salt and pepper.

Mix the bread crumbs and the cheese. Dip the chicken pieces in the egg and then in the bread-cheese mixture, coating each piece well.

Sauté the chicken in the butter over medium heat for about 4 minutes on each side, or until it is well browned all over but still tender.

Pineapple Chicken Wings

4–6 chicken wings
Salt
Freshly ground pepper
1 tablespoon vegetable oil
½ green pepper, cut in strips
1 can (8¼ ounces) crushed pineapple
2 teaspoons soy sauce
1½ cups cooked brown or white rice

Cut the tips off the chicken wings and sprinkle them with salt and pepper. Heat the oil in a skillet. Add the chicken and brown it well on both sides. Remove it from the pan. Sauté the green pepper lightly in the skillet, then put the chicken back in. Mix the undrained pineapple and the soy sauce and pour it over the chicken. Cover the pan and simmer for 30 minutes, or until the chicken is tender. Serve it with hot rice.

Roast Duck Bigarade

Save this for some special occasion: it makes an elegant meal for two.

1 duck (3–4 pounds)
Salt
Freshly ground pepper
1 orange, unskinned, coarsely chopped
1 cup orange juice
⅓ cup honey

Cut the wing tips off the duck. Make a stock by simmering them with the giblets and the neck in 1½ cups of water for about 30 minutes. Strain and reserve the broth for making the sauce.

Meanwhile, preheat the oven to 325° F.

Rub the duck inside and out with salt and pepper. Fill the duck cavity with the chopped orange. Place the duck on a rack in a baking pan and put the pan in the oven. Combine the orange juice and honey and baste the duck frequently while it is roasting. Prick the skin several times to allow the excess fat to escape. Roast the duck according to your preference, allowing 1¼ hours for rare, 1½ hours for medium-rare and about 2 hours for well-done.

Remove the duck to a hot serving platter and keep it warm. Skim the excess fat off the pan juices and proceed to make the sauce:

SAUCE BIGARADE

    Rind of 1 orange
    1 cup hot duck stock (prepared from the giblets)
    1 teaspoon cornstarch
    ¾ cup hot orange juice
    1 tablespoon vinegar
    1 tablespoon sugar
    1 teaspoon lemon juice
    2 tablespoons orange-flavored liqueur (optional)
    Salt
    Pepper
    ½ cup orange sections

Cut the orange rind in matchlike slivers, pour boiling water over it and let it stand for 5 minutes before draining.
Deglaze the baking pan with the reserved duck stock and
thicken it over medium heat with the cornstarch, into
which a little of the stock has been mixed. Stir in the
orange rind, orange juice, vinegar, sugar, lemon juice and,
if desired, Curaçao. Season to taste with salt and pepper.
Simmer the sauce over low heat for about 5 minutes, stirring occasionally. Pour it over the duck and garnish the
duck with the orange sections.

Duckling Varsovia

1 duckling (3–4 pounds), in quarters
Salt
Pepper
1 small head red cabbage (about ¾ pound)
2 tablespoons lemon juice
1½ ounces salt pork, diced
1 small onion, chopped
2 teaspoons flour
¼ cup red wine vinegar
1 tablespoon caraway seeds
2–3 teaspoons light brown sugar
¼ cup dry white wine

Preheat the oven to 375° F.

Wash the pieces of duck and dry them on absorbent
paper. Put them in a shallow baking pan, season them with

salt and pepper, and roast them in the oven until they are well browned.

Meanwhile, shred the cabbage and blanch it by pouring boiling water over it and letting it soak for about 15 minutes. Drain and sprinkle it with the lemon juice.

Sauté the salt pork in a Dutch oven until it gives off some fat. Add the onion and continue to cook over low heat until the pork and the onion are lightly browned. Blend in the flour and cook for a minute or two. Then stir in the vinegar, caraway seeds, brown sugar and wine. Add the drained cabbage, season with some salt and pepper and stir well. Bring it to a boil, cover and simmer for about 20 minutes, adding more liquid only if necessary.

Put the browned duckling pieces on the cabbage in the Dutch oven. Pour off the fat from the baking pan, add a few tablespoons of hot water to the pan and deglaze it by scraping up all the brown bits from the bottom. Pour this over the duckling pieces, cover the Dutch oven and simmer for about 1½ hours, or until the duck is tender, adding a little water if needed and adjusting the seasonings.

Serve the duck on a hot platter surrounded by the cabbage.

Glazed Rock Cornish Hens with Pecan Stuffing

2 Rock Cornish hens
½ onion, chopped
3 tablespoons chopped celery
6 tablespoons butter or margarine
¼ teaspoon salt
Pinch of paprika
2 cups diced stale bread
½ cup chopped pecans
3 tablespoons chopped parsley
Salt
Freshly ground pepper
1 tablespoon cornstarch
½ cup beef broth

Preheat the oven to 425° F.

Thaw the Cornish hens if they are frozen.

To prepare the stuffing: sauté the onion and celery in 3 tablespoons of the butter for about 5 minutes, then add the salt, paprika, bread, pecans and parsley and toss lightly.

Stuff the hens with the pecan stuffing, secure the cavities with toothpicks and tie the legs together. Put the hens in a shallow roasting pan. Melt the remaining butter and pour it over them. Sprinkle with salt and pepper. Roast them for 1 to 1¼ hours, basting several times with the pan drippings.

Mix a little cold water into the cornstarch, then add it gradually to the hot broth, using enough to thicken it. Use this to glaze the hens before you take them from the oven.

Roast Turkey

Turkey is not only a universal favorite, it's also inexpensive and it goes very far. Of course, even the small birds seem large when you are cooking for two, but you can still have the pleasure of cooking a whole turkey because the left-over meat freezes well and there are many fine dishes to make with cooked turkey.

This basic recipe for roast turkey is followed by some suggestions as to what to do with the leftovers. An 8-pound turkey will serve two with enough meat left over for three or four other recipes.

Preheat the oven to 325° F.

Wash the thawed turkey inside and out, and pat it dry. Stuff it, if you wish. Fasten the neck skin to the back of the turkey with a skewer. Tie the legs together with heavy string. Fold the wings back and tie them close to the body. Brush the entire bird with melted butter or margarine.

Put the turkey on its back on a rack in a shallow roasting pan. Roast it uncovered, basting it frequently with the pan drippings. When the turkey begins to turn golden brown, cover it loosely with a tent of foil to prevent excessive browning.

Allow about 20 minutes of cooking time per pound for a small unstuffed turkey, 25 minutes if the turkey is stuffed. If you are using a meat thermometer, insert it in the thickest part of the thigh muscle without touching the bone and roast to an internal temperature of 185° F. An 8-pound turkey should cook in about 3 to 3½ hours. Test for doneness by seeing if the drumstick moves up and down easily and if the thickest part of the drumstick feels very soft when pressed or pinched. Let the turkey stand for about 30 minutes before you carve it.

Serve the turkey with the degreased pan juices, which may be thickened with some flour mixed with a little liquid. Sweet potatoes, green vegetables and cranberry sauce are the traditional accompaniments.

Turkey Divan

1 package (10 ounces) frozen broccoli spears
4 generous slices leftover turkey
2 tablespoons butter or margarine
2 tablespoons flour
1 cup milk or broth, or a mixture of both
1 tablespoon sherry
Salt
Freshly ground pepper
Freshly grated Parmesan cheese

Preheat the oven to 400° F.

Cook the broccoli according to package directions. Drain and arrange it in a small baking dish. Put the turkey slices on the broccoli.

Melt the butter in a small saucepan, blend in the flour and cook for a minute or two before adding the milk or broth. Cook over medium heat, stirring, until the sauce has thickened. Add the sherry and season to taste with salt and pepper.

Pour the sauce over the turkey and broccoli. Sprinkle generously with Parmesan cheese and bake for 15 to 20 minutes, until lightly browned.

Turkey Sukiyaki

2 tablespoons vegetable oil
½ cup finely diced green pepper
½ cup thinly sliced celery
½ pound mushrooms, sliced
½ cup green onions in 1-inch pieces, including tops
1–1½ cups diced leftover turkey
2 tablespoons soy sauce

Heat the oil in a skillet over medium heat. Cook the vegetables in the oil for about 6 to 8 minutes, or until they are barely tender. Stir in the turkey and the soy sauce,, heat it all through and serve it at once.

This dish is good with rice or noodles.

Individual Turkey Pies

2 tablespoons butter or margarine
2 tablespoons flour
¼ teaspoon salt
Pinch of ground sage
Freshly ground pepper
1 teaspoon lemon juice
⅔ cup turkey or chicken broth
1 cup diced leftover turkey
Sherry
Enough dough or mix for half of a 1-crust pie

Melt the butter in a saucepan, blend in the flour, salt, sage and pepper, and cook for a minute or two over low heat. Add the lemon juice and the broth and cook over medium heat, stirring from time to time until the sauce has thickened. Add the turkey, more salt if necessary and a teaspoon or so of sherry according to taste.

Preheat the oven to 425° F.

Pour the turkey mixture into two individual casseroles. Divide the pastry in half and roll it out to fit the top of each casserole. Set the pastry tops in place, trim them and flute the edges. Cut a gash or two in the pastry to allow steam to escape. Bake for 15 to 20 minutes, until the tops are golden brown and the turkey mixture is hot.

Mushroom Turkey Salad

10 mushrooms, washed and sliced
1–1½ cups diced leftover turkey
⅓ cup diced celery
1 tablespoon sliced radishes
1 tablespoon minced green onion
1 teaspoon chopped parsley
2 teaspoons lemon juice
2 tablespoons olive or vegetable oil
¼ teaspoon salt
Pinch of crumbled savory leaves
Freshly ground pepper

Combine the mushrooms, turkey, celery, radishes, green onion and parsley in a mixing bowl. Blend the rest of the ingredients in a separate bowl, pour the dressing over the salad and toss lightly. Chill well before serving.

Turkey Sandwiches

Leftover turkey makes good sandwiches. Try combining slices of turkey with some of the following: leftover stuffing, cranberry sauce, sliced tomatoes, Russian or Thousand Island dressing, American cheese, pickle relish, almonds.

You can also make Turkey Club Sandwiches. Use 3 slices of bread for each sandwich. Toast the bread, then spread one slice with butter and cover it with sliced turkey. Spread both sides of the second slice of toast with mayonnaise or Russian dressing and put it on top of the meat. Place 2 slices of tomato and 2 slices of crisp bacon on the second slice. Add some lettuce, if you wish. Then spread the third slice of toast with mayonnaise and cover the sandwich. Fasten with toothpicks and cut the sandwich diagonally in four triangles.

FISH

Fish is an excellent choice when cooking for two because many seafood dishes can be prepared quickly and easily and there is no problem about buying fish in small enough quantities. Small fish can be bought whole, and larger fish can be cut into fillets or steaks of the appropriate size. For two people, allow a total of ½ to ¾ pound of fish fillets, 1 pound of fish steaks or 1½ pounds of whole fish.

You can use either fresh or frozen fish in these recipes. You should cook frozen fish as soon as it has thawed and *never* refreeze it. Fresh fish should of course also be cooked as soon as possible, and it should be very fresh when purchased. You can tell the freshness of a fish by its smell, its bulging eyes and its firm flesh. A fresh fish will float when placed in cold water.

Fish may be baked, broiled, sautéed, poached or steamed. Whatever the method, take care not to overcook the fish. It is done when the flesh flakes easily and is no longer transparent.

Trout with Anchovy Sauce

Flour
Salt
Freshly ground pepper
2 small whole trout, cleaned
Olive or vegetable oil
4 tablespoons butter or margarine
2 anchovy fillets, cut fine
About ¼ cup white wine
2 tablespoons chopped parsley
Juice of ½ lemon

Season the flour with salt and pepper. Roll the fish in it.

Heat enough oil to cover the bottom of a skillet and pan-fry the fish, about 5 minutes on each side.

Meanwhile, melt the butter in a small saucepan, add the anchovies and heat them for about 5 minutes. Add the wine, parsley and lemon juice and simmer for about 3 minutes more. Taste for seasonings.

Put the fish on a hot platter and pour the sauce over them before serving.

Sole in Vermouth

½–¾ cup dry domestic vermouth
½–¾ pound sole fillets
2 egg yolks
5 tablespoons butter or margarine
2 teaspoons heavy cream
Salt
Freshly ground pepper

Heat the vermouth in a skillet large enough to hold the fish. Wrap the fillets loosely in cheesecloth and poach them in the vermouth for about 10 minutes, until they are cooked through. Remove the fillets from the cheesecloth, put them on a broiler-proof platter and keep them warm.

Boil the vermouth until it is reduced to about ⅓ of a cup. Put it in the top of a double boiler and gradually add the egg yolks, butter and cream. Cook over hot (not boiling) water, stirring, until the sauce just begins to thicken. Do not allow it to boil, or the eggs will curdle. Season the sauce with salt and pepper, pour it over the fish and brown very quickly under the broiler before serving.

Portuguese-Style Codfish

2 tablespoons olive or vegetable oil
¾ cup thinly sliced onions
1 cup cooked rice
½ pound cod fillets
1½ cups canned tomatoes, drained (reserve juice)
¾ teaspoon salt
¼ teaspoon paprika
Freshly ground pepper
Pinch of ground cumin
Pinch of ground cloves
2 teaspoons lemon juice

Preheat the oven to 350° F.

Heat the oil in a skillet and sauté the onion slices until they are soft and lightly browned. Put the rice in a small baking dish and top it with the onions and the fish.

In a small saucepan, combine the rest of the ingredients. Add about ¼ cup of the reserved juice from the tomatoes and heat it all, breaking up the tomatoes with a spoon. Pour the sauce over the fish in the baking dish and bake for about 30 minutes, until the fish is cooked through.

Poached Fish, Sicilian Style

2 slices halibut, swordfish or other thick fish (about
    ¾–1 pound)
2 tablespoons olive oil
2 teaspoons chopped parsley
1 small clove garlic, minced
¼ cup white vinegar
1½ cups canned tomatoes, puréed in blender
Salt
Freshly ground pepper
½ pound fresh peas, shelled, or 1 can (8½ ounces)
    baby peas

Brown the fish quickly in a skillet in hot oil. Add the
parsley, garlic and vinegar and cook until the liquid has
almost evaporated. Add the tomatoes, salt and pepper.
Simmer, covered, for about 20 minutes. Add the peas and
continue to simmer, covered, for 10–15 minutes more.

To serve, place the fish on a hot platter and pour the
sauce over it.

Baked Fish Fillets
with Vegetables

2 medium carrots, scraped and thinly sliced
Salt
1 onion, sliced
2 ribs celery, thinly sliced
Freshly ground pepper
½–¾ pound fish fillets, fresh or frozen
Light cream
Butter or margarine
Paprika

Cook the carrots in a small amount of boiling salted water until they are just tender. Drain them.

Preheat the oven to 425° F.

Arrange the onion slices in the center of a small shallow baking dish and top them with the celery. Sprinkle with salt and pepper and add the carrots. Season the fish fillets on both sides with salt and pepper and place them on top of the vegetables.

Pour in a little cream, enough to cover the bottom of the dish and part of the vegetables. Do not cover the fish. Dot the fish with butter and sprinkle it with paprika. Bake for about 20 minutes.

Fish Fillets Amandine

4 tablespoons butter or margarine
¾ pound fish fillets, fresh or frozen
Salt
Freshly ground pepper
3 tablespoons halved blanched almonds
2 teaspoons lemon juice

Melt 2 tablespoons of the butter in a skillet. Season the fillets with salt and pepper and sauté them quickly until the fish is browned on both sides and flakes easily with a fork. Transfer the fish to a hot platter and keep it warm.

Melt the remaining butter in the same skillet and brown the almonds lightly in it. Add the lemon juice to the almonds and pour it all over the fish. Serve at once.

Fish Rolls
with Celery-Tomato Sauce

1 cup sliced celery
1 can (8 ounces) tomato sauce
2 tablespoons diced green pepper
½ small onion, in thin rings
¼ teaspoon oregano
1 small bay leaf
Pinch of garlic powder
Salt
½–¾ pound flounder fillets, fresh or frozen
Freshly ground pepper

Preheat the oven to 350° F.

Combine the celery, tomato sauce, green pepper, onion rings, 2 tablespoons of water, oregano, bay leaf and garlic powder in a small saucepan. Bring it all to a boil, cover the pot and simmer the sauce for about 10 minutes. Add salt to taste.

Sprinkle both sides of the fillets with a little salt and pepper. Roll them up and arrange them in a small shallow baking dish. Pour the sauce over them and bake them for about 30 minutes.

Fish Mornay

½–¾ pound flounder or cod fillets, fresh or frozen
1 tablespoon butter or margarine
1 tablespoon flour
¼ teaspoon salt
Freshly ground pepper
¾ cup milk
Freshly grated Parmesan cheese

Bring a small amount of salted water to a boil in a skillet and poach the fish in it until it flakes easily with a fork. Drain the fish, cut it into serving pieces, arrange them in a small broiler-proof dish and keep them warm.

Melt the butter in a small saucepan, blend in the flour and cook for a minute or two, stirring constantly with a whisk. Add the salt and some pepper. Add the milk and cook, stirring, until the sauce has thickened. Remove the sauce from the heat and stir in about 2 tablespoons of grated cheese. Taste and adjust the seasonings.

Pour the sauce over the fish and sprinkle generously with additional cheese. Broil until the top is lightly browned.

Poached Salmon Steaks with Egg Sauce

1 tablespoon white vinegar or lemon juice
2 teaspoons salt
1 small onion, sliced
Few sprigs fresh dill or parsley
4 peppercorns
2 small salmon steaks, fresh or frozen

Put 3 cups of water in a skillet large enough to hold the salmon steaks. Add the vinegar, salt, onion, dill and peppercorns and bring it to a boil. Carefully add the salmon steaks and bring to a boil again. Cover the skillet and simmer the salmon for about 8 minutes, until the fish flakes easily with a fork (do not overcook). Use a slotted spoon to remove the salmon to a hot platter.

Make the sauce while the salmon is simmering:

Egg Sauce

> 1 tablespoon butter or margarine
> 2 teaspoons flour
> ¼ teaspoon salt
> Dash of white pepper
> ½ cup milk or cream
> ½ teaspoon prepared mustard
> 1 sliced hard-cooked egg

Melt butter over low heat. Add the flour, salt and pepper and cook for a few minutes, stirring constantly. Add the milk, stirring with a whisk, and cook over medium heat until the sauce is smooth and thickened. Stir in the mustard and the sliced egg. Serve with the poached salmon.

Broiled Salmon with Herbs

2 small salmon steaks, about ¾-inch thick
2 teaspoons grated onion
Juice of 1 lemon
3 tablespoons butter or margarine, melted
½ teaspoon salt
Freshly ground pepper
¼ teaspoon marjoram
1 tablespoon chopped watercress or chives
1 tablespoon finely chopped parsley

Place the fish on a greased broiler rack. Combine the rest of the ingredients and pour half of the mixture over the fish. Broil for about 6 minutes under medium heat. Turn the fish and pour the remaining sauce over it. Broil for 5 or 6 minutes longer.

Lord Baltimore Crab Cakes

½ pound crab meat
¾ teaspoon salt
½ teaspoon white pepper
½ teaspoon dry mustard
1 teaspoon Worcestershire sauce
1 egg yolk
½ teaspoon chopped parsley
Mayonnaise
1 egg, beaten
Fine dry bread crumbs
Vegetable oil

Combine the crab meat, salt, pepper, mustard, Worcestershire sauce, egg yolk and parsley. Shape the mixture into 2 large cakes or 4 small cakes, and add a little mayonnaise, if necessary, to bind it. Dip the cakes in the beaten egg and then in the bread crumbs, coating them well. Fry them quickly in a little bit of hot oil until they are browned.

Coquilles St. Jacques
(Scallops in Shells)

½ pound bay or sea scallops
Butter or margarine
2 shallots or green onions, chopped
Bouquet garni (some parsley, celery, thyme and bay leaf
    tied in a cheesecloth bag)
½ cup dry white wine
Salt
4–6 mushrooms, chopped
1 tablespoon lemon juice
Freshly ground pepper
1½ tablespoons flour
1 egg yolk
⅓ cup heavy cream
Freshly grated Parmesan cheese
Bread crumbs

Dry the scallops on paper towels. Place them in a saucepan with 1 tablespoon of butter, the shallots and the *bouquet garni*. Barely cover with the white wine, and season
with a little salt. Bring the wine to the boiling point, cover
the pot and simmer *very gently* for 4 or 5 minutes, or until
the scallops are just tender. Drain and save the broth for
the sauce. If large, cut the scallops in small pieces and set
them aside.

Melt a little butter in the same pan and sauté the mushrooms in it for a minute. Add 2 tablespoons of water, the
lemon juice and a dash of salt and pepper. Simmer the

mushrooms gently for a few minutes, then drain, combining the mushroom liquid with the reserved liquid from the scallops.

Prepare a *beurre manié* by kneading the flour with 1½ tablespoons of butter, working them together into small balls the size of peas. Heat the combined liquids from the scallops and the mushrooms and gradually stir in the *beurre manié*, one ball at a time. Cook and stir until the sauce is thickened and smooth, then cook for 2 or 3 minutes more.

Add the scallops and heat them through. Beat the egg yolk with the cream, add the mixture to the sauce and cook gently, stirring, until the sauce is thick and smooth. Do not let it boil. Add the mushrooms and adjust the seasonings if necessary.

Spoon the scallop mixture into individual ramekins or shells, sprinkle them with Parmesan cheese and bread crumbs, and brown lightly under the broiler before serving.

Creole Jambalaya

2 tablespoons butter or margarine
¼–½ pound smoked ham, coarsely diced
1 onion, chopped
1 clove garlic, minced
1 small green pepper, coarsely diced
1½ cups drained, canned tomatoes
1½ cups meat or chicken broth
1 small bay leaf, crushed
Pinch of dried thyme
Pinch of chili powder
Freshly ground pepper
¾ cup uncooked rice
½ pound fresh or frozen shrimps, shelled, cleaned and
  cooked

Melt the butter in a casserole or Dutch oven. Add the ham,
onion, garlic and green pepper and cook until lightly
browned. Add the tomatoes, broth, bay leaf, thyme, chili
powder and pepper and bring it all to a boil. Stir in the
rice, cover and simmer for about 30 minutes, or until the
rice is tender and the liquid is absorbed. Adjust the seasoning and add the shrimps before serving.

Shrimp Curry

1–2 tablespoons vegetable oil
1 medium onion, diced
⅓ cup diced celery
1 can (8 ounces) tomatoes, drained
1 teaspoon curry powder
Pinch of turmeric
1 small bay leaf
¾ cup chicken broth
2 teaspoons flour
Lemon juice
Salt
Freshly ground pepper
½ pound fresh or frozen shrimps, peeled and cleaned
1½ cups hot cooked rice
Chutney
1 large banana, sliced

Heat the oil in a saucepan, add the onions and sauté until they are soft and golden. Add the celery and tomatoes and sauté for about 5 minutes more. Sprinkle with the curry powder and turmeric, then add the bay leaf and the broth. Stir well. Cover the pan and simmer for about 45 minutes. Remove the bay leaf.

Blend the flour with a small amount of water and stir it into the hot sauce. Simmer until the sauce has thickened, adding a little more broth if it seems too thick. Season to taste with a little lemon juice, salt and pepper, and add more curry powder if you wish.

Add the shrimps, bring to a boil and simmer for just a few minutes, until the shrimps are cooked through but not overcooked.

Serve with rice, chutney and sliced banana.

VEGETABLES

These recipes call for vegetables that are fresh, rather than frozen or canned, because it is easier to buy fresh ones in just the right amounts for two people. Fresh vegetables, properly treated, also taste better and are relatively inexpensive if you buy them in season.

Instead of stocking up, buy only what vegetables you need and cook them soon afterward. If they are kept for a while they may still be crisp, but they will lose flavor as time passes. It is also best not to rinse vegetables until you are ready to cook them, or you will wash away flavor.

Many people think they dislike vegetables, because they are usually overcooked and served in a soggy or mushy state. They *should* be crisp and firm; avoid too much cooking at all costs. Whether boiled, steamed, baked or just cooked fast in a little bit of water, vegetables should be tested frequently and cooked only until they are just tender. Undercooked vegetables will still taste good, but overcooked vegetables are a disaster. Because they have more flavor, fresh vegetables need less seasoning than frozen or canned, so don't be too liberal with the salt and pepper.

Since a second cooking destroys vegetables, don't reheat leftovers. This is another good reason for buying small quantities. If you should have some left over, try serving them cold in a vinaigrette dressing.

Fresh Vegetable Medley

2 new potatoes, peeled
1 cup vegetable, meat or chicken bouillon
2 medium carrots, halved lengthwise and cut in 2-inch
  pieces
¼ pound green beans, in ½-inch pieces
¼ cup celery, in 1½-inch pieces
1 tomato, halved
1–2 teaspoons butter or margarine

Put the potatoes in a saucepan with ½ cup of the bouillon
and bring it to a boil. Cook, uncovered, for 5 minutes, then
cover and simmer for 15 minutes, or until tender. In another saucepan, cook the carrots and beans in the remaining bouillon, uncovered, for 5 minutes. Cover and cook for
5 more minutes. Add the celery and cook for 5 minutes
longer.

Meanwhile, dot the tomato halves with the butter and
broil them to the desired degree of doneness. Arrange the
tomatoes on a serving plate and surround them with the
drained vegetables. Reserve the broth for soup.

Asparagus Hollandaise

¾ pound asparagus

Break or cut off the tough ends of the asparagus stalks. Using a vegetable parer, peel the lower part of the spears to remove the scales and coarse skin. Wash the asparagus well in warm water.

Bring about 1 inch of salted water to a boil in a large skillet. Add the asparagus and boil, uncovered, for about 5 minutes. Cover the skillet and cook briskly, testing frequently with a fork, for about 10 minutes longer, until the asparagus spears are barely tender. Drain thoroughly, put on a hot serving dish and serve with Hollandaise Sauce, which should be warm, not hot, and may be made about 30 minutes in advance.

HOLLANDAISE SAUCE

> **½ cup butter or margarine**
> **3 egg yolks**
> **1–1½ tablespoons lemon juice**
> **Salt**
> **Dash of cayenne or white pepper**

Melt the butter over hot water in the top part of a double boiler and heat it until it is very hot. Put the egg yolks, lemon juice, salt and pepper in a small bowl and beat them with a beater or wire whisk for a minute or so. Gradually beat the hot butter into the egg-yolk mixture. Beat in 2 tablespoons of hot water.

Scrape the mixture back into the top of the double boiler and put it over hot water. Do not let the water in the bottom boil or touch the pot above. Stir constantly with the whisk for a few minutes until the sauce is slightly thickened. (If the sauce should curdle, remove it from the stove and gradually beat in 1 tablespoon of hot water.) Let the sauce stand off the stove but over warm water until you are ready to serve the asparagus.

Jerusalem Artichokes

½–¾ pound Jerusalem artichokes
Salt
Freshly ground pepper
Butter or margarine
Lemon juice
Chopped parsley

The Jerusalem artichokes should be firm and free from blemishes. Wash, peel, and slice them. Cook in a small amount of lightly salted boiling water for 10 to 20 minutes, or until the artichokes are just tender. Drain and season them with pepper, butter and a little lemon juice. Sprinkle with chopped parsley before serving.

Stir-Fried Green Beans

This recipe is a lovely way to add variety to green beans.
Save the extra water chestnuts from the can to use for
Rumaki (page 16).

2 tablespoons peanut or vegetable oil
½ pound green beans, in 2-inch lengths
2 green onions, in 2-inch lengths
5–6 mushrooms, thinly sliced
2 ounces water chestnuts, drained and thinly sliced
1 teaspoon cornstarch
½ teaspoon sugar
1½ tablespoons soy sauce
3 tablespoons chicken broth
Salt

Heat the oil in a skillet. Add the beans, green onions,
mushrooms and water chestnuts and stir-fry until they are
all well coated with the oil. Mix the cornstarch, sugar,
soy sauce and chicken broth, and pour the mixture over
the vegetables. Mix well, cover the skillet and cook over
medium heat, stirring occasionally, for about 10 minutes,
or until the beans are barely tender. Season to taste with
salt.

Broccoli Vinaigrette

3 teaspoons red-wine vinegar
3 tablespoons olive or salad oil
Salt
Freshly ground pepper
1 teaspoon minced parsley
1 teaspoon minced green pepper
1 teaspoon minced chives
½ teaspoon minced capers
1 pound broccoli, washed and cooked

Combine all the ingredients except the broccoli in a small jar. Shake well and pour over the cooked broccoli. Serve chilled or at room temperature.

Brussels Sprouts with Tarragon-Mustard Sauce

½ pound (1 pint) Brussels sprouts, washed and trimmed
1 tablespoon finely chopped onion
2 teaspoons butter or margarine
2 teaspoons flour
¼ teaspoon dry mustard
⅛ teaspoon tarragon leaves, crushed
½ cup chicken broth or bouillon
1½ teaspoons vinegar

Cook the sprouts in a small amount of lightly salted boiling water until they are just tender. Drain them.

Sauté the onion in the butter until it is tender but not browned. Stir in the flour, mustard and tarragon, and cook for a minute or so. Add the broth and vinegar and cook, stirring, until the sauce is thickened and smooth. Pour the sauce over the sprouts and serve at once.

Deviled Cabbage with Almonds

1 small head cabbage (about 1 pound), coarsely shredded
Salt
1 tablespoon butter or margarine
1 tablespoon flour
1–2 teaspoons Dijon-style mustard
½ cup milk
3 tablespoons slivered almonds, lightly toasted

Put the cabbage, 1½ teaspoons of salt and 2 or 3 tablespoons of boiling water in a pot or saucepan. Cover the pot and cook over low heat, stirring once or twice, for about 10 minutes, or until the cabbage is crisp-tender. Drain.

Melt the butter in a small saucepan. Blend in the flour, mustard and ¼ teaspoon of salt. Cook for a minute, then stir in the milk and cook, stirring, over medium heat until the sauce thickens.

Preheat the oven to 400° F.

Put the cabbage in a small casserole. Add the sauce and then the almonds. Cover and bake for about 20 minutes, or until thoroughly heated. Uncover and bake for 5 minutes more to crisp the almonds.

Sweet-Sour Red Cabbage

½ onion, chopped
1 tablespoon butter or margarine
1 small red cabbage (about 1 pound), shredded
1 small tart apple, peeled and diced
1 tablespoon cider vinegar
1 tablespoon brown sugar
1 teaspoon caraway seed
½ teaspoon salt
Freshly ground pepper
2 tablespoons seedless raisins

Using a small casserole, cook the onion in the butter for
about 5 minutes. Add the cabbage, cover and cook for
about 5 minutes more. Add ⅓ cup water, and the rest of
the ingredients. Cover and simmer for about 10 minutes.

Ginger Carrots

3 or 4 medium carrots, scraped and cut in ½-inch slices
1 teaspoon lemon juice
½ teaspoon salt
¼ teaspoon ground ginger
Dash of pepper
1 tablespoon butter or margarine

Preheat the oven to 400 °F.

Put the carrots in a small buttered casserole. Mix the lemon juice with the salt, ginger and pepper. Pour it over the carrots and dot them with butter. Cover and bake for 1 hour, adding a little more butter if necessary, until the carrots are tender.

Braised Celery

2 celery hearts
Chicken broth, white wine or a combination of both
Salt
Dash of hot-pepper sauce
1–2 tablespoons butter or margarine
Freshly ground pepper

Trim the celery and cut off the tops, reserving them for making soup or stock. Split the hearts in half and wash them very well. Put them in a skillet and barely cover with broth or wine. Add salt and hot-pepper sauce to taste, bring to a boil, cover and reduce the heat. Cook, turning once or twice, until the celery is just tender. Drain off the broth, reserving it for some other use.

Place the celery, cut side down, in the skillet and add butter and pepper to taste. Heat well, turning once. Serve hot.

You may also cool the drained celery and serve it cold with a vinaigrette sauce.

Tiny Corn Pancakes

1 cup fresh-corn pulp (from 6 ears fresh corn) or
   1 can (8 ounces) cream-style corn
1 egg, separated
¼ teaspoon salt
Freshly ground pepper
2 tablespoons flour
2 tablespoons shortening

To prepare pulp from fresh corn, slit down the center of each row of kernels with a sharp knife. Then, using the dull edge of a table knife, scrape out the pulp and milky juice.

In a mixing bowl, combine the corn pulp, beaten egg yolk, salt, pepper and flour. Mix well. Beat the egg white until it is stiff but not dry and fold it gently into the corn mixture.

Heat the shortening in a skillet. Drop the batter by heaping tablespoonfuls into the hot shortening and brown the pancakes on both sides. Serve at once with meat or fish. You will have 12 to 18 pancakes.

Ratatouille Provençale

1 very small eggplant
¼ cup olive oil
1 can (8 ounces) plum tomatoes, drained
2 pimientos, drained
1 onion, sliced
1 small clove garlic, minced
1 tablespoon chopped parsley
½ teaspoon capers
Salt
Freshly ground pepper

Peel the eggplant and cut it in cubes. Sauté the cubes in the oil in a skillet for a few minutes. Add the tomatoes, pimientos, onion, garlic, parsley and capers, and salt and pepper to taste. Cook slowly, mixing occasionally, for about 20 minutes, or until the eggplant is cooked. Do not cook too long, or the vegetables will become mushy.

Baked Green Peppers and Onions

1 cup sliced green peppers
1 cup sliced onions
1 tablespoon butter or margarine
Salt
Freshly ground pepper

Preheat the oven to 350° F.

Put the peppers, onions and butter in a small casserole. Season to taste with salt and pepper. Cover the casserole and bake until the vegetables are done to your preference.

Sautéed Parsnips

¾ pound parsnips
Salt
Butter or margarine
Freshly ground pepper

Peel the parsnips and cook them in a small amount of lightly salted water until they are tender. Drain and cool, then slice them lengthwise, about ¼-inch thick.

Sauté the slices in butter until they are golden brown on both sides. Season to taste with freshly ground pepper.

Stuffed Baked Potatoes

2 baking potatoes
⅓ cup small-curd creamed cottage cheese
1 egg, beaten
Salt
Freshly ground pepper
1 tablespoon chopped chives or green onions
Melted butter or margarine
Paprika

Preheat the oven to 450° F.

Scrub the potatoes and bake them for 45 to 50 minutes, or until they are done. Cut a slice from the top of each potato and scoop out the inside. Mash the potato well, then beat in the cottage cheese, egg, salt and pepper to taste, and chopped chives. Pile the mixture back into the shells, rounding it slightly. Brush the tops with a little butter, then put the potatoes back in the oven for about 10 minutes or so. If they are not lightly browned, put them under the broiler for a few minutes. Sprinkle with paprika before serving.

Pommes Anna

1 pound potatoes
About 4 tablespoons butter or margarine, melted
Salt
Freshly ground pepper

Peel the potatoes and slice them ⅛-inch thick. Rinse in cold water and dry them well.

Preheat the oven to 425° F.

Butter a pie pan well. Line the bottom of the pan with a piece of brown paper cut from a bag to fit it, then grease the paper. Arrange a layer of overlapping slices of potato in the pan, starting in the middle and making concentric circles out to the edge. Pour about 1 teaspoon of melted butter over the layer and sprinkle it with salt and pepper. Add more layers of potatoes, buttering and seasoning each layer. Cover the pie pan with foil and bake on the bottom shelf of the oven for about 50 minutes, or until fork-tender.

Drain off the butter and save it for some future use. Carefully turn the potatoes upside down on a round plate and peel off the paper. If the potatoes are not well browned, put them under the broiler for a few minutes.

Potatoes à la Huancaina

This dish from the Peruvian Andes is named after the town of Huancayo.

½ cup diced Cheddar cheese
1½ tablespoons vegetable oil
¼ cup milk
1 tablespoon lemon juice
Dash of hot-pepper sauce
Salt
Freshly ground pepper
1½–2 cups diced cooked potatoes, hot or at room
   temperature
1 hard-cooked egg
Chopped black olives

Heat the cheese, oil and milk in the top of a double boiler over simmering water. Stir until the cheese is melted. Remove the pot from the heat and stir in the lemon juice and pepper sauce. Season to taste with salt and pepper. Put the potatoes in a serving dish, pour the sauce over them and garnish with sliced egg and chopped olives.

Hot Potato Salad

2 potatoes, boiled in their jackets
2 slices bacon
1 hard-cooked egg, diced
½ onion, finely diced
2 teaspoons cider vinegar
Salt
Freshly ground pepper
Chopped parsley

Peel the potatoes and slice them ¼-inch thick. Fry the bacon in a skillet until it is crisp. Drain the bacon and crumble it.

Pour off most of the bacon fat. Heat the remaining drippings in the skillet and add the potatoes, bacon, egg, onion and vinegar. Season to taste with salt and pepper. Mix gently and heat through. Serve hot, sprinkled with parsley.

This dish is good with frankfurters or sausages.

Wilted Spinach

4 slices bacon
2 tablespoons cider vinegar
½ teaspoon sugar
2 cups washed and torn fresh spinach leaves
  (about ¼ pound)

Sauté the bacon until it is crisp. Drain and crumble it.
Pour off all but 2 tablespoons of the fat in the pan. Add
1 tablespoon of water, the vinegar and sugar, and heat.
Pour over the spinach and toss well. Top with the crumbled bacon and serve at once.

Squash Casserole

1 pound small zucchini or summer squash, or both
Salt
Freshly ground pepper
1–2 tablespoons butter or margarine
1 tablespoon bread crumbs
1–2 tablespoons freshly grated Parmesan cheese
1 clove garlic, halved

Preheat the oven to 350° F.

Wash the squash, cut it into ½-inch pieces, and put it
in a shallow baking dish or pie pan. Sprinkle with salt and
pepper to taste and add about 1 tablespoon of water. Dot
with butter, then sprinkle with the bread crumbs and
cheese. Put each of the garlic halves on toothpicks and
push them into the mixture in the dish. Bake for 45 minutes, or until the vegetables are tender. Remove the garlic
before serving.

Honey-Glazed Acorn Squash

1 medium acorn squash
2 tablespoons butter or margarine, melted
¼ teaspoon salt
¼ teaspoon allspice
2 tablespoons honey

Preheat the oven to 350° F.

Wash the squash and cut it in half. Remove and discard the seeds and stringy fibers. Put the squash, cut side down, in a shallow baking dish and add ½-inch of hot water. Bake for 45 minutes, or until fork-tender. Remove the squash and pour off the water.

Turn the squash cut side up. Mix the butter, salt, allspice and honey and put half the mixture on each squash half. Bake, basting with the glaze, for about 15 minutes.

Country-Fried Hubbard Squash

This dish can be made with acorn squash or pumpkin, if you prefer.

2 cups peeled, sliced squash, in ¼-inch slices
¼ cup sliced onion
2 tablespoons vegetable oil
Salt
Freshly ground pepper

Cook the squash and onion slices for a few minutes in the oil in a heavy skillet. Season to taste with salt and pepper. Cover the skillet and cook over medium heat, turning 2 or 3 times, for about 10 minutes, or until the squash is lightly browned and tender. Uncover and cook, continuing to turn, for 5 or 10 minutes longer, until the squash is evenly browned.

DRIED BEANS, PASTA and RICE

Dried beans and peas, pasta and rice are staples in every well-stocked home. When you are cooking for two, they are particularly useful because they can be measured out in exactly the right small quantity for one meal. These dry products will keep almost indefinitely and they are nutritious, relatively inexpensive and readily available in a great variety of shapes and forms. Basically bland, dried beans, rice and pasta are amenable to many different kinds of seasonings and preparation methods.

Many of the dishes in this section make hearty meals in themselves. Others, intended as side dishes, can easily be converted to main courses with the addition of some leftover cooked meat or vegetables. In these recipes the quantity to use for two people varies according to the amount of other ingredients in a dish and the nature of the dish itself. In general, we suggest generous amounts. These dishes are cheap and popular, and if there *are* any leftovers, they will keep well and be even better the second time around.

DRIED BEANS

Some of these dried bean dishes—Black Beans with Rice, Chili Con Carne, Tomato-Cheese Soy Beans—are intended as main courses. Others—New England Baked Beans, Baked Lentils with Bacon—are side dishes, but with the addition of some cut-up cooked frankfurters or sausages, they can easily be converted into full meals. If you wish to increase the quantity of the beans a bit, remember that ½ cup of dried beans or lentils becomes 1 to 1¼ cups when cooked.

Dried beans and peas usually come in 1-pound packages, the equivalent of 2 cups. Of the endless variety available, some of the more common ones are black beans, pinto beans, red and white kidney beans, lima beans, marrow beans, navy or pea beans, Great Northern beans, soy beans, lentils, chickpeas, split peas and black-eyed and yellow-eyed peas. It is fun to experiment with different kinds of beans. Try substituting one variety for another in these recipes.

Although soaking will do them no harm, split peas, lentils and those beans that are marked "quick-cooking" do not require presoaking. All other beans should be washed and then soaked overnight in cold water, allowing three times as much water as beans. As an alternative to overnight soaking, the washed beans may be boiled for 2 minutes and then left to stand, covered, for an hour.

After soaking is completed, beans should be cooked until they are tender. Always use the soaking water to prevent any loss of nutrients. Cook them slowly, so that the beans do not break. If you wish, you may add a little butter to the cooking water to keep the foam down.

Cooking time for dried beans and peas varies, according to the age of the beans and where they were grown. You can tell when the beans are done by tasting them or by seeing if the skin breaks when you blow on them.

Cooked bean and pea dishes will keep well in the refrigerator for several days. They also freeze well, so if space is available, cook extra quantities and freeze them for future use.

Black Beans with Rice

For a change from meat dishes, serve this as a hearty main course instead.

½ cup (¼ pound) dried black beans
½ teaspoon salt
1 slice bacon, finely diced
½ onion, finely chopped
2 tablespoons finely chopped green pepper
1 small clove garlic, minced
Pinch of thyme leaves
Red-wine vinegar
Salt
Freshly ground pepper
1½ cups hot cooked rice
1 pimiento, in strips
1–2 tablespoons chopped sweet onion
1 hard-cooked egg, chopped

Wash the beans and drain them. Soak them in 2 cups of cold water overnight, or cover them with 2 cups of water, boil for 2 minutes and then let them stand, covered, for 1 hour.

Bring the beans in the soaking water to a boil, add the salt, cover the pot and simmer for about 1½ hours, or until the beans are tender.

While the beans are cooking, sauté the bacon in a skillet until it is lightly browned, then pour off all but a tablespoon or so of the bacon fat. Cook the onion, green pepper, garlic and thyme in the bacon grease, stirring occasionally, for about 10 minutes.

When the beans begin to get tender, add the sautéed vegetables and simmer, covered, for about 1 hour, until the beans are quite soft and the sauce is a deep rich color. Add about 1 teaspoon of vinegar and season to taste with salt and pepper.

To serve, put a generous helping of hot cooked rice on each plate and a ladleful of black beans to one side. Garnish the beans and rice with pimiento strips, chopped onion and chopped egg.

New England Baked Beans

½ cup (¼ pound) dried pea or navy beans
1 slice lean bacon, in quarters
1 small onion, peeled
¼ teaspoon salt
2 tablespoons light molasses
¼ teaspoon dry mustard
1 teaspoon light-brown sugar

Wash the beans and drain them. Soak them in cold water overnight, or cover them with 2 cups of water, boil them for 2 minutes and then let them stand, covered, for 1 hour.

Bring the beans in the soaking water to a boil, cover and simmer for about 1 hour or until the beans are tender, adding more water if necessary. Drain them, reserving the liquid.

Preheat the oven to 300° F.

Put the beans in a small baking dish or bean pot. Bury the bacon pieces and the onion in the beans. Mix ⅓ of a cup of the reserved liquid with the salt, molasses, mustard and brown sugar. Pour the mixture over the beans, adding more of the reserved liquid, if necessary, to just cover them. Cover the dish and bake for 6 to 8 hours, leaving the dish uncovered for the last hour.

Michigan Baked Beans

½ cup (¼ pound) dried Great Northern beans or
    white kidney beans
1 tablespoon butter or margarine
1 tablespoon packed brown sugar
1 tablespoon molasses
2 tablespoons chili sauce
1 can (8 ounces) tomatoes, drained and cut up
½ onion, thinly sliced
¼ teaspoon dry mustard
½ teaspoon salt

Wash the beans and drain them. Soak them in cold water overnight, or cover them with 2 cups of water, boil them for 2 minutes and then let them stand, covered, for 1 hour.

Bring the beans in the soaking water to a boil, cover the pot and simmer for about 1 hour, or until the beans are tender. Drain them, reserving the liquid.

Add the butter to ⅓ of a cup of the reserved liquid, then add the rest of the ingredients. Mix well with the beans and pour it all into a small shallow baking pan or very small bean pot. Cover and bake in a 325° F. oven (not preheated) for about 1½ hours. Add a little more of the reserved liquid if necessary. Uncover and bake for 15 minutes longer, or until the liquid is cooked down but the beans are still juicy.

Baked Lentils with Bacon

⅓ cup dried lentils
2 slices bacon, diced
¼ teaspoon salt
½ cup tomato sauce or tomato purée
1 teaspoon prepared mustard
2 teaspoons molasses

Wash the lentils and put them in a small pot. Brown the bacon lightly and drain it. Add it to the lentils, together with the salt and 1 cup of water. Bring it all to a boil, cover the pot and simmer for 30 minutes, or until the lentils are tender but not mushy.

Preheat the oven to 250° F.

Mix together the tomato sauce, mustard and molasses. Add the mixture to the lentils, stir well and pour it all into a small baking dish. Cover and bake for about 2 hours, until most of the liquid has been absorbed.

Chili Con Carne

⅓ cup dried pinto beans
½ pound round or other lean beef, in ½-inch cubes
1–2 tablespoons olive oil
1 small bay leaf
1½ teaspoons chili powder
½ teaspoon salt
1 clove garlic, minced
¼ teaspoon crushed cumin seeds
¼ teaspoon oregano
1 teaspoon paprika
2 teaspoons corn meal
2 teaspoons flour

Wash the beans and drain them. Soak them in cold water overnight, or cover them with 1½ cups of water, boil them for 2 minutes and then let them stand, covered, for 1 hour.

Bring the beans in the soaking water to a boil, cover and simmer them until they are tender, adding more water if necessary. Drain them.

Sear the meat in hot oil. Add 1 cup of water, cover, bring to a boil and let simmer for 1 hour. Then add the bay leaf, chili powder, salt, garlic, cumin, oregano and paprika and simmer for ½ hour more. Remove the bay leaf.

Blend the corn meal and flour with a little cold water to make a paste. Stir it into the meat mixture and simmer until it thickens, for about 10 minutes. Add more salt and chili powder to taste. Add the beans and heat thoroughly.

Try serving this with hot rice and a crisp green salad.

Tomato-Cheese Soy Beans

This is a tasty and nourishing meatless main course. Serve it with a green salad and crisp bread.

⅓ cup dried soy beans
¾ cup cooked corn kernels
1 cup canned tomatoes, undrained, in pieces
¼ teaspoon sugar
½ teaspoon salt
Freshly ground pepper
¼ cup bread crumbs
2 tablespoons butter or margarine, melted
3 tablespoons grated Cheddar cheese

Wash the beans and drain them. Soak them in cold water overnight, or cover them with 2 cups of water, boil them for 2 minutes and then let them stand, covered, for 1 hour.

Bring the beans in the soaking water to a boil, cover and simmer them for 1 to 1½ hours, or until they are tender. Drain them and arrange them in the bottom of a shallow baking dish.

Preheat the oven to 375° F.

Arrange a layer of the corn on the beans in the baking dish. Mix the tomatoes, sugar, salt and pepper, and pour the mixture over the beans and corn. Top with the crumbs, drizzle with the butter and sprinkle with the cheese. Bake, uncovered, for 30 to 45 minutes.

PASTA

Each of these pasta dishes, served with a salad and some Italian bread, makes a complete meal. We suggest serving generous portions: ½ pound of pasta may seem like a lot for two people, but it quickly disappears. Many people seem to have a great capacity for eating pasta, but if there *should* be some left over, it is very good reheated.

In addition to being cheap and universally popular, many pasta dishes are also quick and easy to prepare. Pasta comes in many different shapes and sizes; use them interchangeably in these recipes for variety.

Boil at least 2 quarts of salted water to cook ½ pound of pasta and keep the water boiling briskly throughout the cooking process. If you are cooking long spaghetti which does not fit in the pot, hold the ends in the boiling water until they soften enough for you to work the spaghetti into the water. Stir with a fork a few times to keep the noodles from sticking together.

Do not overcook pasta; it should be chewy, or *al dente*, as the Italians say. This is especially true if the pasta is to be further cooked by combining it with a sauce and then baking it. If you cook pasta ahead and wish to hold it for a while before serving it, moisten it with a little butter, oil or sauce to keep it from drying out or sticking together.

Spaghetti with Meat Sauce

1–2 tablespoons olive oil
¼ cup chopped onion
1 small clove garlic, minced
¼ pound mushrooms, washed and sliced
½ pound ground lean beef
1 can (16 ounces) tomato purée
1–2 tablespoons tomato paste
¼ cup dry red wine
¼ teaspoon salt
¼ teaspoon oregano leaves
¼ teaspoon basil
Freshly ground pepper
Sugar
⅓–½ pound spaghetti
Freshly grated Parmesan cheese

Heat the oil in a skillet and add the onion and garlic. Cook them, stirring from time to time, until they are tender. Add the mushrooms and cook for about 5 minutes more. Mix in the ground meat and brown it, breaking it up with a fork, until it is just cooked through. Pour off any excess grease from the pan.

Add the rest of the ingredients except the spaghetti. Cover the skillet and simmer the sauce for at least 40 minutes, longer if possible. Adjust the seasonings as it simmers, adding a little sugar if the tomatoes are too acid, and more oregano, salt and pepper to taste.

Cook the spaghetti in boiling salted water until it is just tender. Serve it with the sauce and with freshly grated Parmesan cheese.

Mushroom-Spaghetti Casserole

4 tablespoons butter or margarine
¼ cup bread crumbs
2 tablespoons flour
1¼ cups milk
Salt
Freshly ground pepper
Sherry
¼ pound spaghetti
¼ pound mushrooms, washed, sliced and sautéed in a
   little butter
1 or 2 hard-cooked eggs, sliced
Freshly grated Parmesan cheese (optional)

Melt the butter in saucepan. Add 2 tablespoons of the melted butter to the bread crumbs, mix well and set aside.

Blend the flour into the remaining 2 tablespoons of butter in the pan and cook for a minute or two, stirring constantly. Gradually add the milk and cook over medium heat, stirring, until the sauce is smooth and thickened. Season to taste with salt, pepper and a teaspoon or two of sherry.

Preheat the oven to 350° F.

Cook the spaghetti in boiling salted water until it is just

tender; drain it. Arrange the spaghetti in a shallow buttered baking dish and add the mushrooms and sliced egg. Season with salt and pepper and pour the sauce over all. Sprinkle with the bread-crumb mixture and some grated Parmesan cheese, if you wish. Bake for about 30 minutes or until heated through and bubbly.

Ziti with Zucchini-Beef Sauce

½ pound ground beef
1 small clove garlic, minced
½ pound small zucchini, diced
½ cup diced green pepper
1 tomato, quartered
1 can (8 ounces) tomato sauce or tomato purée
½ teaspoon salt
Freshly ground pepper
¼ teaspoon oregano
¼ teaspoon basil
⅓–½ pound ziti (wide macaroni)

Brown the beef, together with the garlic, in its own fat in a skillet. Pour off any excess grease. Add the zucchini, green pepper, tomato and tomato sauce and cook over medium heat for about 5 minutes, or until the ingredients are well mixed. Season with the salt, pepper, oregano and basil, cover the skillet and simmer the sauce for about 30 minutes. Adjust the seasonings to taste.

Cook the ziti in boiling salted water until it is just tender. Drain it and serve it with the zucchini sauce.

Spaghetti with Clam Sauce

2 tablespoons olive oil
Few sprigs parsley, chopped
1 small clove garlic, minced
½ teaspoon salt
⅛ teaspoon pepper
1 tablespoon minced onion
1 can (8 ounces) minced clams, undrained
⅓–½ pound spaghetti

Heat the oil in a heavy saucepan. Add the parsley and garlic and sauté for a few minutes. Add the salt, pepper, onion and clams and stir together well.

Cook the spaghetti in boiling salted water; drain it. Toss it in the clam sauce and reheat, if necessary, before serving.

Green Noodles alla Carbonara

1 tablespoon butter or margarine
½ cup diced cooked ham
Freshly grated Parmesan cheese
2 tablespoons evaporated milk
1 egg, well beaten
¼ teaspoon salt
⅓–½ pound green spinach noodles

Melt the butter in a skillet and sauté the ham in it until crisp and brown; set aside.

Combine 3 tablespoons of Parmesan cheese with the milk, egg and salt. Cook the noodles in boiling salted water and drain them. Add the ham to the cheese mixture and toss it with the hot noodles. Serve at once with additional Parmesan cheese.

Turkey or Ham Tetrazzini

2 tablespoons butter or margarine
2 tablespoons flour
¼ teaspoon salt
Dash of hot-pepper sauce
Freshly ground pepper
¾ cup milk
½ cup turkey or chicken broth
1 egg yolk
2 tablespoons heavy cream
1–2 tablespoons sherry
8 medium mushrooms, washed, sliced and sautéed in
    a little butter
1½ cups diced cooked turkey or ham
¼ pound thin spaghetti
¼ cup freshly grated Parmesan cheese

Melt the butter in a saucepan and stir in the flour. Cook for a minute or two, stirring constantly, and add the salt, hot-pepper sauce and pepper. Gradually add the milk and broth and cook over medium heat, stirring, until the sauce is smooth and thick. Beat the egg yolk with the cream and add it very gradually to the sauce, stirring it over low heat until it is heated through. Do not let it boil. Add the sherry, mushrooms and the turkey or ham.

Preheat the oven to 375° F.

Cook the spaghetti in boiling salted water until it is barely tender. Drain it and combine it with the turkey or ham sauce. Put it in a shallow buttered baking dish and sprinkle it with the Parmesan cheese. Bake for about 30 minutes, or until the tetrazzini is hot and bubbly.

Lasagna

Since all of the ingredients in this dish are precooked, they can be prepared and assembled well ahead of time.

TOMATO-MEAT SAUCE

> 1 small onion, finely chopped
> 1 small clove garlic, minced
> 1–2 tablespoons olive oil
> 6 ounces ground beef
> 1 can (8 ounces) tomatoes
> 3–4 ounces tomato paste
> ¾ teaspoon salt
> Dash of cayenne
> ¼ teaspoon sugar
> Pinch of basil
> ½ small bay leaf

Cook the onion and garlic in hot olive oil until they are tender. Add the ground beef to the skillet and brown it lightly. Pour off any excess fat. Add the rest of the ingredients and ¾ cup of water. Simmer, uncovered, for 1 hour or more, until the sauce is well integrated. Remove the bay leaf, taste the sauce and adjust the seasonings. Makes 2 cups.

Preheat the oven to 325° F.

4 ounces lasagna noodles (4 large noodles)
Salt
Olive oil
½–¾ cup ricotta cheese
3 ounces mozzarella cheese, sliced
4 tablespoons grated Parmesan cheese

Put the noodles in a pot of boiling water to which some salt and olive oil have been added, and cook them until they are just tender. Drain them. Arrange the ingredients in a buttered bread pan or small baking dish, making two layers each of noodles, ricotta, mozzarella, tomato sauce and Parmesan cheese. Bake for about 45 minutes, until the lasagna is hot and bubbly.

Creamy Macaroni and Cheese

Make half of this recipe if you wish to serve it as a side dish.

4 ounces elbow macaroni
1½ tablespoons butter or margarine
2 tablespoons flour
Pinch of dry mustard
½ teaspoon salt
Freshly ground pepper
1½ cups milk
¼ teaspoon Worcestershire sauce
1 tablespoon grated onion (optional)
4–5 ounces sharp cheese, shredded
3 tablespoons bread crumbs
2 tablespoons butter or margarine, melted

Cook the macaroni in boiling salted water until it is barely tender. Drain and put it in a small buttered casserole.

Preheat the oven to 375° F.

Melt the butter in a saucepan and stir in the flour, mustard, salt and pepper. Cook for a minute or two, then stir in the milk. Cook over medium heat, stirring constantly, until the sauce is smooth and thickened. Add the Worcestershire sauce, onion and cheese and stir until the cheese begins to melt. Pour the cheese sauce over the macaroni and stir lightly.

Mix the bread crumbs with the butter and sprinkle them over all. Bake for 20 to 30 minutes, until hot and bubbly.

Cheese-Spinach-Noodle Casserole

1 package (10 ounces) frozen leaf spinach, cooked and
    well drained
4 ounces wide noodles, cooked and drained
1 egg
¼ cup milk
¼ cup coarsely shredded sharp Cheddar cheese
½ cup creamed cottage cheese
¼ teaspoon salt
Freshly ground pepper
Pinch of nutmeg

Preheat the oven to 375° F.

Grease a small shallow baking dish. Spread the spinach
in the bottom and cover it with the noodles. Beat the egg
and milk together and stir in the rest of the ingredients.
Mix well. Pour the mixture over the noodles and bake for
about 30 minutes, or until set.

RICE

All of these rice dishes are intended to be served as side dishes, but many of them can be converted into main courses with the addition of some cooked meat, fish, poultry or vegetables.

Rice, when cooked, expands to three times its volume. These recipes call for ½ cup of uncooked rice which will yield 1½ cups of cooked rice, ample for a side dish for two people. If you are adding other ingredients and serving the rice as a main course, you may want to cook a bit more rice as well.

Brown rice can be substituted for white rice in any of these recipes. It is high in food value and provides good flavor and texture. Brown rice takes a bit longer than white rice to cook and has a greater yield: ½ cup of uncooked brown rice will expand to 2 cups of cooked brown rice. Minute Rice, on the other hand, takes less time to cook and also produces less: ½ cup of uncooked Minute Rice will produce 1 cup of cooked rice.

There are many different ways to cook rice. Some people vary the methods they use, others stick to one way which works well for them. Whatever the method, here are certain general rules to follow:

Do not add cold water to rice while it is cooking.

Always keep the water boiling, or the rice will be soggy.

Do not stir rice while it is cooking or remove the lid from the pan while it is simmering.

Do not wash rice before or after cooking, or much of its food value will be lost.

Rice Pilaf

If you add about a cup of shredded cooked pot roast to this pilaf, you will have a main-course dish.

2 tablespoons butter or margarine
1 small onion, chopped
½ cup uncooked rice
1 cup chicken or beef broth

Melt the butter in a skillet and sauté the onion in it until it is lightly browned. Add the rice and sauté it until it is golden. Stir in the broth (and pot roast, if you wish), and bring it to a boil. Cover the skillet and simmer over low heat, without stirring, for about 20 minutes, or until the rice is cooked and the liquid absorbed.

Cheese Risotto

½ cup chopped onion
2 tablespoons butter or margarine
½ cup uncooked rice
1 can (8 ounces) tomatoes, cut up and drained
  (reserve liquid)
1 chicken bouillon cube
6 mushrooms, sliced
Boiling water
½ cup shredded sharp Cheddar cheese

Sauté the onion in the butter in a skillet. When the onion is tender, add the rice and cook it, stirring, until it is very lightly browned. Add the tomatoes, bouillon cube and mushrooms. Add enough boiling water to the reserved tomato liquid to make 1 cup and stir it into the rice mixture. Bring to a boil and stir until the bouillon cube is dissolved. Cover the skillet and simmer for about 20 minutes, without stirring, until the rice is tender and all the liquid is absorbed.

When the rice is done, add the cheese and stir it in gently until it has melted. Serve at once.

Fried Rice

This rice makes an excellent side dish with a roast or chops. If you add about a cup of diced, cooked pork or chicken, it will be a meal in itself.

1–2 tablespoons chopped green onion
1½ tablespoons vegetable or peanut oil
1½ cups cooked rice
1 egg
½–1 tablespoon soy sauce

Sauté the onion in the oil until it is wilted. Add the rice (and meat, if you wish) and cook, stirring, for about 5 minutes. Beat the egg with the soy sauce and add it to the rice mixture. Cook, stirring, until the egg is set.

Spanish Rice

1 small onion, chopped
½ green pepper, chopped
2 tablespoons butter or margarine
½ cup uncooked rice
1 small bay leaf, crumbled
1 clove
½ teaspoon salt
½ teaspoon sugar
Freshly ground pepper
1 can (8 ounces) tomatoes, cut up and drained
    (reserve liquid)
Boiling water

Sauté the onion and green pepper in the butter until they are tender. Add the rice and cook until lightly browned. Add the bay leaf, clove, salt, sugar, pepper and tomatoes. Add enough water to the reserved tomato liquid to make 1 cup and add it to the pan. Bring to a boil and simmer, covered, for about 20 minutes, without stirring, until the rice is cooked and all the liquid has been absorbed.

Yellow Rice

½ cup uncooked rice
1 cup boiling water
¾ teaspoon salt
½ teaspoon turmeric
1 tablespoon butter or margarine

Preheat the oven to 350° F.

Put the rice in a small casserole. Add the water, salt, turmeric and butter. Cover and bake for about 1 hour, until the rice is done.

Curried Raisin Rice

¼ cup chopped onion
3 tablespoons butter or margarine
½ cup uncooked rice
1½ teaspoons curry powder
1 cup chicken broth
½ teaspoon salt
¼ cup raisins

Cook the onion in the butter until it is tender. Add the rice and continue to stir until the rice and onion are golden. Add the curry powder and stir it in well. Add the broth, salt and raisins and bring it all to a boil. Cover the skillet, reduce the heat and simmer, without stirring, for 20 minutes, or until the rice is done and the liquid is absorbed.

Rice Salad

½ cup uncooked rice
1 cup boiling water
Olive or vegetable oil
Vinegar
Salt
Freshly ground pepper
¼ pound bel paese cheese, cubed
6 radishes, sliced
1 tablespoon chopped walnuts
About ⅓ cup chopped watercress

Cook the rice in the salted water and drain it. While it is still warm, toss with equal parts of oil and vinegar and season it to taste with salt and pepper. Chill.

Just before serving, add the cheese, radishes, walnuts and watercress and toss well.

CHEESE
and EGGS

Cheese and eggs are versatile raw ingredients on which a cook can always rely. They are especially useful to those who cook in small quantities, because they keep well and are available in the small amounts needed.

Eggs and cheese can be used in just about any kind of dish imaginable and at any time of day. They are frequently used in breakfast, lunch and dinner dishes, and in snacks, desserts and sauces. Eggs and cheese are also good to eat without embellishment—what better treat than a piece of cheese or a hard-cooked egg with salt?

Many egg and cheese dishes can be assembled quickly. They are high in protein and economical. Best of all, they are lovely to look at and delicious to eat.

CHEESE

Cheeses are produced in infinite varieties all over the world. Today, many exotic cheeses are available in ordinary supermarkets as well as in numerous specialty stores.

It is always fun to experiment with new cheeses and to make new discoveries.

Swiss and Cheddar are probably the most popular all-purpose cheeses. Like Parmesan and Romano, they may be grated on top of casseroles, and are good for melting, as are muenster and mozzarella. Try Roquefort, Stilton or blue cheese as appetizers; cream or cottage cheese for breakfast or lunch; sliced Swiss or muenster cheese with sandwich meats; and Brie, Camembert, Boursin or bel paese with fruit for dessert (see also "Desserts," page 230).

Cheese keeps well in the refrigerator, hard cheese longer than soft. Wrap it well, covering the cut surfaces completely so that they do not dry out. Cheese can also be frozen. Natural cheese, such as Cheddar or Swiss, will keep in the freezer for about six weeks, processed cheeses for about four months. Thaw them overnight in the refrigerator and use them soon afterward.

Eggs

An endless number of good, simple and often elegant dishes are made with eggs. Many of these dishes should be made at the last minute and served immediately, which makes them difficult to prepare for *twelve* people but perfect when you are cooking for just two.

Eggs are delicate and should always be cooked gently. They will have better volume and texture if they are brought to room temperature before they are used.

Try to buy eggs when they are as fresh as possible. There is a world of difference between the rich flavor of a fresh egg and the flat taste of an old one.

Double-Cheese and
Mashed-Potato Pie

---

1 cup firm mashed potatoes
¼ cup finely diced mozzarella cheese
¼ cup finely diced sharp Cheddar cheese
1 egg, well beaten
1 teaspoon chopped parsley or chives
Freshly ground pepper
2 tablespoons slivered almonds
Butter or margarine

Preheat the oven to 400° F.

Combine and mix well the potatoes, mozzarella cheese, Cheddar cheese, egg, parsley and pepper. Put the mixture in a small buttered pan or baking dish and sprinkle it with the almonds. Dot with butter and bake for about 15 minutes, until the pie is puffy and golden brown.

Cottage-Cheese Soufflé

1½ tablespoons butter or margarine
1½ tablespoons minced green onion
1½ tablespoons flour
¾ teaspoon salt
Freshly ground pepper
¾ cup milk
¾ cup small-curd creamed cottage cheese, drained
3 eggs, separated

Preheat the oven to 350° F.

Heat the butter in a saucepan and sauté the onion in it for about 5 minutes, until it is tender. Blend in the flour, salt and pepper and cook for a minute or two. Gradually add the milk and cook it over medium heat, stirring, until the mixture is smooth and thick. Remove the pot from the heat and stir in the cheese.

Add the egg yolks, one at a time, to the cheese mixture. Beat the egg whites until they form soft peaks. Carefully fold the cheese mixture into the egg whites. Pour into a buttered 1-quart soufflé dish and bake for about 30 minutes, until the soufflé is puffed and brown and the center is not loose when you shake it. Serve it immediately.

Cheese-Spinach Pie

---

1 box (10 ounces) frozen chopped spinach
1 cup cottage cheese
2 eggs, beaten
1 teaspoon caraway seed
1 teaspoon salt
Freshly ground pepper
Dash of nutmeg
2 tablespoons freshly grated Parmesan cheese
Butter or margarine

Preheat the oven to 350° F.

Cook the spinach and drain it very well. Put it in a bowl and add the cottage cheese, egg, caraway seed, salt, pepper and nutmeg. Mix it all together well.

Put the mixture in a small shallow buttered baking dish. Sprinkle it with the Parmesan cheese and dot it with butter. Bake for about 20 minutes, until the pie is set.

Cheese Spoon Bread

½ cup corn meal
¾ teaspoon salt
Freshly ground pepper
2 teaspoons sugar
1½ tablespoons butter or margarine
1½ cups milk
¾ cup water
6 ounces American cheese
2 eggs, beaten

Preheat the oven to 325° F.

Put the corn meal, salt, pepper, sugar and butter in a saucepan. Add ¾ cup of milk and the water. Bring to a boil and cook over medium heat, stirring, until thickened. Cut two thirds of the cheese into small pieces and stir it into the corn meal mixture. Add the remaining milk and the eggs, and mix well.

Pour the mixture into a 1-quart casserole or into two individual baking dishes. Slice the remaining cheese and put it on top of the dish or dishes. Bake for 35 to 40 minutes.

Cottage Eggs with Rice

1 cup cooked rice
3 hard-cooked eggs
¼ cup cottage cheese
1 tablespoon mayonnaise
Salt
Freshly ground pepper
2 tablespoons butter or margarine
1 tablespoon minced onion
2 tablespoons flour
1 cup milk
Paprika

Preheat the oven to 350° F.

Put the cooked rice in a shallow baking dish. Slice the eggs in half lengthwise, remove the yolks and mash them with the cottage cheese and mayonnaise. Season to taste with salt and pepper and fill the whites with the mixture. Arrange the stuffed eggs on the rice.

Melt the butter in a saucepan and cook the onion in it for a few minutes, until it is tender. Stir in the flour and cook over low heat for a few minutes more. Gradually stir in the milk. Cook over medium heat, stirring, until the sauce has thickened. Season it to taste with salt and pepper.

Pour the sauce over the eggs and sprinkle with a little paprika. Bake, uncovered, for about 20 minutes, or until heated through.

Onions and Eggs

3 hard-cooked eggs
1 cup chopped onions
3 tablespoons butter or margarine
¼ cup dry white wine
¼ teaspoon salt
Freshly ground pepper
Dash of paprika
Pinch of dry mustard
2 tablespoons chili sauce
3 tablespoons bread crumbs

Preheat the oven to 425° F.

Slice the eggs and put them in a small buttered baking dish. Brown the onions lightly in 2 tablespoons of butter and add the wine, salt, pepper, paprika, mustard and chili sauce. Stir well and pour the mixture over the eggs. Sprinkle with the crumbs, dot with the remaining butter and bake for about 15 minutes, until heated through.

Thousand-Island Eggs

½ cup sour cream
¼ cup chopped stuffed olives
1 tablespoon chopped chives
¼ cup catsup
Salt
Freshly ground pepper
Dash of garlic salt
Dash of hot-pepper sauce
4 teaspoons butter or margarine
4 eggs

Preheat the oven to 350° F.

Mix the sour cream, olives, chives, catsup, salt, pepper, garlic salt and pepper sauce. Place 2 teaspoons of butter in each of two individual casseroles, and put the dishes in the oven until the butter melts and gets very hot. Remove the casseroles from the oven and break two eggs into each dish. Cover the eggs with the sour-cream mixture, using half for each casserole. Bake for 15 to 20 minutes.

Shirred Eggs in Tomato Shells

2 large ripe tomatoes
Salt
Freshly ground pepper
⅛ teaspoon dried dill
2 eggs
1 slice lean bacon, fried crisp and crumbled
2 tablespoons bread crumbs

Slice the tops from the tomatoes, scoop out the pulp and reserve it for some other use. Season the inside of the tomato shells with salt, pepper and dill.

Preheat the oven to 400° F.

Break an egg into each tomato shell. Mix the bacon and the bread crumbs and sprinkle half of the mixture on each filled tomato shell. Bake for about 20 minutes.

Egg-Potato Skillet

2 tablespoons butter or margarine
1½–2 cups peeled, sliced potatoes
1 small onion, thinly sliced
Salt
Freshly ground pepper
3 eggs, lightly beaten
1 tablespoon chopped parsley

Melt the butter in a skillet and add the potatoes and onion slices. Lift and turn them with a wide spatula until they are well coated with the butter. Sauté, turning them, for a few minutes. Season with salt and pepper, cover the skillet and continue cooking, turning them from time to time, until the potatoes are browned and tender.

Pour the eggs over the top of the potatoes and onions and sprinkle it all with parsley. Cover and cook over low heat for 5 to 10 minutes, or until the eggs are set.

Swiss Eggs

1 tablespoon butter or margarine
½ cup light cream
4 eggs
Salt
Hot-pepper sauce
Shredded Swiss cheese
Buttered toast
1½ tablespoons sherry

Melt the butter in a medium skillet and add the cream. Heat until the cream bubbles. Break in the eggs very carefully, seasoning each with salt and a dash of hot-pepper sauce. Poach over low heat until the whites are nearly set. Sprinkle them generously with the cheese. Cook the eggs until the whites are set. Remove the eggs and put them on the toast.

Add the sherry to the cream in the skillet and cook for ½ minute. Pour the sauce over the eggs.

Plain French Omelet for Two

4 eggs
¼ teaspoon salt
Dash of freshly ground pepper
2 tablespoons butter or margarine

Break the eggs into a medium bowl and add 1 tablespoon of cold water and the salt and pepper. Beat the eggs briskly for 25 to 30 seconds, just enough to blend the yolks and whites.

Melt the butter in a 9- or 10-inch omelet pan or skillet with sloping sides. Using moderate heat, wait until the butter begins to foam (do not let it brown) and then add the eggs.

The entire cooking time for the omelet will be about 3 or 4 minutes. Hold the handle of the pan in your left hand (if you are right-handed) and a fork in your right. As the edges of the omelet crinkle and look firm, lift them and push them toward the center with the fork so that the uncooked egg runs under the firm portion. Tilt the pan as necessary with your left hand to hasten the flow of the egg. Continue lifting the egg with the fork until all the uncooked egg has run under the cooked portion. Smooth the top of the omelet with the fork. The edges should look firm and the top moist and creamy. Lift the edge of the omelet with a metal spatula; if the bottom is not lightly browned, increase the heat slightly.

Using a spatula, fold the omelet in half or in thirds and slide it onto a serving plate. Serve at once.

Filled French Omelet

If you wish to fill a French omelet, put the filling down the center before folding the first third over it. The filling should be warm or at room temperature. If you have extra filling, pour it over and around the omelet just before serving.

In addition to various omelet fillings, ingredients can be added directly to the eggs before they are cooked. Some suggestions: finely chopped herbs, such as parsley, chives, basil or tarragon; sautéed minced onion; sautéed finely-chopped mushrooms. Some people like to sprinkle grated Cheddar or Parmesan cheese on an omelet just before it is done.

CHICKEN-LIVER FILLING

> 1 green onion, sliced
> 3 or 4 small mushrooms, washed and sliced
> 2 tablespoons butter or margarine
> ½ pound chicken livers, cut up
> 1 teaspoon flour
> 2 tablespoons dry white wine
> Salt
> Freshly ground pepper

Sauté the onion and the mushrooms in the butter in a skillet. When they are tender, push them to the side and add the livers. Cook, stirring, until the livers are just cooked through. Mix the livers in with the onion and mushrooms, and sprinkle the mixture with the flour. Stir in the

wine and heat gently, stirring, until the filling is slightly
thickened. Season to taste with salt and pepper.

Fill an omelet for two with some of the chicken-liver
filling and put the remainder of the filling around the sides.

ONION-BACON FILLING

> 4 green onions with some of the green tops,
>   thinly sliced
> 2 tablespoons butter or margarine
> ¼ pound bacon, cooked until crisp and then
>   crumbled

Sauté the onion in the butter in a skillet until it is just
tender. Combine it with the crumbled bacon and fill
an omelet for two.

HAM-POTATO FILLING

> 1 small onion, sliced
> 2 tablespoons butter or margarine
> ½ cup chopped cooked potato
> ½ cup chopped cooked ham
> Salt
> Freshly ground pepper

Sauté the onion in the butter in a skillet until it is tender.
Add the potato and the ham and sauté them until they are
lightly browned. Season the mixture to taste with salt and
pepper.

Fill an omelet for two with some of the ham-potato filling and serve the remainder around the sides.

FILLING FOR SPANISH OMELET

> 2 tablespoons minced onion
> ¼ cup minced green pepper
> 2 tablespoons butter or margarine
> 1 can (8 ounces) tomato sauce
> 1 teaspoon sugar
> 1 teaspoon Worcestershire sauce
> Dash of cayenne

Sauté the onion and green pepper in the butter in a saucepan until they are tender. Add the tomato sauce, sugar, Worcestershire sauce and cayenne, bring it all to a boil and then simmer for 15 minutes or more, until the sauce has thickened slightly.

Fill an omelet for two with some of the sauce, fold the omelet and pour the remaining sauce over the top.

DESSERTS

These desserts for two are simple to prepare in very small quantities. Many of them use fruit, cheese or custard as the basic ingredient. They are light desserts—proper conclusions to full and satisfying meals.

Layer cakes and pies—the heavier desserts—have their place, too, after a light or casual meal or for special celebrations. On festive occasions, larger pies and cakes, which will serve a crowd, work well.

However, it is also possible to make a small cake for two. (See, for example, our recipe for Nut Torte, page 236.) Make enough batter for one 9-inch cake layer and bake it in an 8-inch square pan. When the cake is cool, cut it in two or three equal pieces which serve as the layers. Ice them, and you will have a small, rectangular layer cake. If you are especially fond of cake, try to buy some 6-inch round layer pans at a bakery supply store. Then you can make two small round layers, using the recipe for one 9-inch layer. Or make cupcakes with half a cake recipe and freeze the extras, if there are any.

Pies can also be made in small sizes. Use one small tart pan for two, or two individual tart shells. Prepare enough dough for a 2-crust pie, form the extra half into a ball, and freeze it. It will keep that way indefinitely. Or use a packaged piecrust mix, taking from the box only what you need at the time.

Remember that pies and cakes in miniature form require less time to bake than larger sizes. Check small ones frequently while they are baking.

There are also many kinds of cookie dough (including commercially prepared, slice-and-bake cookies in a roll) that keep under refrigeration for a very long time. (See our recipe for Walnut Crescents, page 235.) You can slice off what you need and bake it when you wish. You can also bake a full batch of cookies at one time and store the extras. Most cookies keep well in the freezer or in an airtight container, provided you don't stack or enclose them until they have cooled completely.

Baked Apples with Mincemeat

2 large apples
2 teaspoons prepared mincemeat (or mixed raisins
    and chopped nuts)
Grated rind of ½ lemon
Juice of ½ lemon
1 tablespoon light-brown sugar
1 teaspoon honey
Heavy cream (optional)

Preheat the oven to 350° F.

Wash the apples and core them without cutting through the stem end. Hollow out the apples, leaving a shell about ½-inch thick. Chop the apple pulp very fine and mix it with the mincemeat and lemon rind. Fill the apples with the mixture.

Arrange the apples in a small shallow baking dish. Mix the lemon juice with enough water to make about ⅓ of a cup. Pour the liquid into the pan. Sprinkle the apples with the sugar and drizzle them with the honey. Bake, basting occasionally, for about 50 minutes, or until done.

Serve slightly warm, with heavy cream if you wish.

Quick Apple Pie

¼ cup butter or margarine
2 or 3 large apples
¼ cup sugar
¼ cup flour
2 tablespoons chopped nuts
Cinnamon
Whipped cream (optional)

Preheat the oven to 425° F.

Put the butter in the freezer to get it very firm. Peel, core and cut the apples in ½-inch-thick wedges. Put the apples in a greased shallow baking dish with about 1-quart capacity. Combine the sugar and flour and mix them very well. Sprinkle the mixture on top of the apples. Slice the butter thin with a sharp knife and arrange it in a single layer on top. Bake for 20 minutes. Remove the dish from the oven, sprinkle it with nuts and cinnamon to taste and bake for 10 minutes more.

Serve warm, with whipped cream if you wish.

Applesauce

Homemade applesauce should be prepared in the fall, when apples are in season and are cheap and flavorful. Two pounds of apples will make about 3 cups of applesauce. Make large quantities and freeze or preserve most of it for use throughout the year.

Tart cooking apples
Brown sugar
Cinnamon (**optional**)

Wash the apples well. Remove the stems and cut the fruit in quarters or eighths. Put the pieces in a heavy kettle with just a little water in it, enough to cover the bottom. Bring to a boil and simmer, covered, watching very carefully to avoid scorching, until the apples are very tender. Drain the apples and reserve the juice.

Force the apples through a sieve or use a food mill. Discard the skins, seeds and cores. Add some of the reserved apple juice, enough to make an applesauce of the consistency you prefer. Season it to taste with sugar, and with cinnamon if you wish.

Put any extra applesauce in plastic containers and freeze it for future use. Or you can make a preserve by putting the excess back in the pot, bringing it to a boil and pouring it at once into hot sterilized jars, filling to within ½ inch of the top. Stir with a rubber spatula to remove air bubbles, seal at once and process in a boiling-water bath for 25 minutes.

Nut-Laced Applesauce Dessert

1–1½ cups applesauce, preferably homemade (above)
Grated rind of ½ lemon
¼ cup butter or margarine
⅓ cup sugar
½ cup pecans, chopped
1½ teaspoons cornstarch
1 egg, separated

Combine the applesauce and lemon rind and mix well. Put the mixture in a small shallow buttered baking dish.

Preheat the oven to 400° F.

Cream the butter, add the sugar and continue to cream until light and fluffy. Add the nuts, cornstarch and egg yolk and mix well. Beat the egg white until it is stiff, and fold it into the nut mixture. Spoon the mixture on top of the applesauce and spread carefully so that it covers the applesauce completely. Bake for 20 minutes or until the topping is well browned and set. Serve while still warm.

Banana-Berry Dessert

1–2 bananas
1 package thawed frozen strawberries, raspberries or
    mixed fruit

Peel the bananas and cut them in chunks. Put them in a glass serving bowl and top them with the thawed fruit.

Blueberry Meringue Shells

2 egg whites, at room temperature
¼ teaspoon cream of tartar
½ cup sugar
¼ teaspoon vanilla extract
Ice cream
Fresh blueberries or barely thawed frozen dry pack

Combine the egg whites and the cream of tartar in a mixing bowl and beat at high speed until soft peaks form. Gradually add the sugar, beating constantly. Add the vanilla and continue beating until stiff peaks form.

Preheat the oven to 250° F.

Cover a small cookie sheet with brown paper cut to size from a paper bag. Put 4 heaping teaspoonfuls of the beaten egg whites on the paper, at least 2 inches apart, and flatten them to make round bases about 2 inches in diameter. Spoon the remaining mixture around the edge of the bases to a height of about 1½ inches, leaving the centers unfilled. Bake for 1 hour. Turn off the heat and let stand for about 1 hour longer. Remove the shells from the paper and let them cool on a rack. These meringues can be made ahead and stored in an airtight container.

When ready to serve, fill the shells with ice cream and top them with fresh blueberries.

Saucepan Brownies

3 tablespoons butter or margarine
1 square unsweetened chocolate
¼ teaspoon vanilla extract
½ cup sugar
1 egg
⅓ cup flour
⅛ teaspoon salt
⅓ cup chopped nuts

Preheat the oven to 325° F.

Melt the butter and the chocolate in a saucepan over low heat, stirring; let cool. Beat in the vanilla and the sugar. Add the egg, beating well. Stir in the flour and salt and then the nuts. Spread in a small buttered pan or baking dish. Bake for about 15 or 20 minutes, until a toothpick inserted in the center emerges clean. Cool and cut into squares. Makes 8 to 12 brownies, depending on the size of the pan.

Chocolate-Orange Mousse

This delicious dessert is made in a blender and couldn't be easier.

½ teaspoon grated orange rind
2 tablespoons packed light-brown sugar
1 egg yolk
1 egg
3 squares (3 ounces) semisweet chocolate, melted
   and cooled
1½ tablespoons orange juice
½ cup heavy cream

Combine the orange rind, sugar, egg yolk and egg in a blender, and whirl until light and foamy. Add the chocolate, orange juice and cream, and whirl until well blended. Pour into 2 individual dessert dishes and chill for about an hour, until set.

Chocolate-Fudge Batter Pudding

⅓ cup flour
3 tablespoons unsweetened cocoa
¼ teaspoon baking powder
¼ teaspoon salt
⅓ cup sugar
2 teaspoons butter or margarine, melted
¼ teaspoon vanilla
3 tablespoons milk
3 tablespoons chopped pecans or walnuts
½ cup boiling water
Confectioners' sugar
Vanilla ice cream

Blend together the flour, 1 tablespoon of the cocoa, the baking powder and the salt; set aside. Mix half the sugar, the butter and the vanilla in a bowl. Combine the flour mixture with the sugar mixture alternately with the milk, blending well after each addition. Stir in the nuts.

Preheat the oven to 350° F.

Combine the remaining sugar, cocoa and boiling water in a small tart pan or shallow baking dish about 4 or 5 inches in diameter. Drop the batter by tablespoonfuls onto the hot mixture. Do not stir; the batter will bake while the sauce remains liquid. Bake for about 30 to 40 minutes, until the top is crusty. Sprinkle with confectioners' sugar.

Spoon out the cake while it is still warm. Cover it with the sauce from underneath and top with a dab of vanilla ice cream.

Baked Cottage-Cheese Custard

2 eggs
1 cup milk
¼ cup sugar
⅛ teaspoon salt
½ teaspoon vanilla
½ cup small-curd creamed cottage cheese
Nutmeg

Preheat the oven to 350° F.

Beat the eggs until they are blended. Add the milk, sugar, salt, vanilla and cottage cheese. Mix well, then pour into a shallow 2½- to 3-cup baking dish. Sprinkle with nutmeg.

Set the baking dish in another pan and add 1 inch of hot water to the outer pan. Bake for about 1 hour, or until a knife inserted in the center of the custard comes out clean. Serve warm or chilled.

Figs in Apple Juice

½ cup unsweetened apple juice
¼ cup water
½ package (6 ounces) dried figs
1 tablespoon golden raisins

Bring the apple juice and water to a boil. Pour the liquid over the figs and raisins, cover and refrigerate for 24 hours.

Cheese and Fruit

Cheese and fruit go well together and make an easy and refreshing dessert—perfect in an emergency or after a rich or heavy meal.

Some good combinations:
- Blue or Roquefort with pears
- Camembert with plums, fresh pineapple or grapes
- Swiss or cream cheese with oranges or tangerines
- Provolone with green grapes or pears
- Port du Salut with apples
- Brie with pears, peaches or strawberries
- Stilton with bananas or plums
- Gruyère with figs
- Gorgonzola with peaches
- Edam with honeydew melon
- Parmesan with apples or cantaloupe

Fruit in Sour Cream

⅔ cup orange sections
1 banana, peeled and sliced ½-inch thick
1 small unpeeled red apple, diced
1 teaspoon orange liqueur or kirsch
⅓ cup sour cream
Brown sugar

Toss the fruit with the liqueur and chill it. Just before serving, toss with sour cream. Sprinkle each serving with brown sugar.

Ricotta and Fruit

Ricotta cheese
Pecan halves
Pitted dates
Fresh fruit wedges

Put a scoop of ricotta cheese in the center of each individual dessert plate. Arrange some pecan halves, dates and fresh-fruit wedges around the cheese.

Apricot-Brandy Ice Cream

½ pound fresh peaches or 5 ounces frozen peaches
1 tablespoon sugar
½ pint peach ice cream, softened
3 tablespoons apricot brandy

Peel and slice the peaches. Add the sugar and whirl in
a blender. (If you are using frozen peaches, defrost them
before blending and omit the sugar.) Combine the peach
purée with the softened ice cream and stir in the apricot
brandy. Work quickly, especially if the fruit is not cold.
Refreeze in a serving bowl or in parfait glasses for at least
3 hours.

Ice Cream with Chocolate Fudge Sauce

½ cup milk
2 squares unsweetened chocolate
⅛ teaspoon salt
¾ cup sugar
2 tablespoons light corn syrup
1 tablespoon butter
½ teaspoon vanilla
Vanilla, chocolate or coffee ice cream

Heat the milk and the chocolate together over low heat, stirring constantly. Beat until smooth. Add the salt, sugar and corn syrup. Bring it all to a boil and cook, stirring, for 5 minutes. Remove the pot from the heat and stir in the butter and the vanilla. Makes about 1 cup of sauce.

Serve the sauce warm or cold on ice cream. It is also good on cream puffs or on plain cake.

Italian Strawberry Ice

1 cup (½ pint) strawberries
2 tablespoons sugar
2 teaspoons lemon juice

Wash and hull the berries and purée them in a blender. Boil the sugar and 3 tablespoons of water together for 5 minutes. Cool.

Combine the sugar water and the berry purée, then stir in the lemon juice. Freeze, stirring frequently, to a mush, and serve in individual sherbet dishes.

Peach-Rice Betty

1½ cups cooked brown rice
2 peaches, peeled and thinly sliced
3 tablespoons chopped nuts
1 teaspoon lemon juice
3 tablespoons honey

Preheat the oven to 350° F.

Spread half the rice in a buttered 1-quart casserole. Combine the peaches, nuts and lemon juice. Top the rice with half the peach mixture, then add the remaining rice. Top with the remaining peach mixture and drizzle with the honey. Bake for 30 minutes, or until the peaches are soft.

Prunes in Port

6 ounces pitted prunes
½ cup port
1 slice lemon
Plain yogurt

Put the prunes, port, lemon and ½ cup of water in a saucepan. Bring to a boil and simmer for 5 to 10 minutes. Chill.

Serve with yogurt.

Strawberry Whip

1 cup strawberries, washed, hulled and sliced
Dash of salt
1 egg white, at room temperature
1 cup confectioners' sugar

Combine the strawberries, salt, egg white and sugar in a
mixing bowl. Beat until very stiff. Serve plain or as a topping for angel cake or fruit.

Walnut Crescents

*This recipe will make about 30 crescents. You can keep the
dough for quite a few days in the refrigerator, cutting off
pieces to use as you need them. Or you can bake them all
at one time, since they will keep very well in an airtight
container and can also be frozen.*

½ cup butter or margarine, softened
¼ cup confectioners' sugar
1 teaspoon vanilla extract
⅛ teaspoon salt
½ cup chopped walnuts
1 cup minus 2 tablespoons flour

Cream the butter, add the sugar, vanilla and salt and beat until light. Stir in the nuts and the flour and mix very well. Wrap the dough in waxed paper and chill it thoroughly.

Preheat the oven to 300° F.

Divide the dough in four equal parts. Shape each part into thin rolls about ½ inch in diameter, working on a lightly floured board. Cut the rolls in 2-inch pieces, taper the ends and shape each into a crescent. Put them on un-buttered baking sheets and bake for 18 to 20 minutes. Remove to a rack to cool. Sift additional confectioners' sugar over them while they are still warm.

Nut Torte

1 tablespoon flour
1¼ teaspoons baking powder
2 eggs
⅓ cup sugar
½ cup shelled nuts

Preheat the oven to 350° F.

Butter well two 6-inch round layer pans or one 8-inch square pan.

Mix the flour and the baking powder. Put the eggs and the sugar in a blender and whip them until they are frothy and smooth. Add the nuts and blend until they are grated fine. Add the flour mixture and whirl until it is all well mixed. Pour the batter into the pans and bake for

about 20 minutes, or until a knife inserted in the center
comes out clean. Cool completely.

If you have used a square pan, cut the cake into thirds
to make three layers. Put filling between the layers and on
the top and sides.

Chill the filled cake until you are ready to serve it.

FILLING

½ teaspoon freeze-dried coffee
1 teaspoon vanilla
¾ cup heavy cream
3 tablespoons sugar

Dissolve the coffee in the vanilla. Whip the cream until it
begins to thicken, then add the coffee mixture and the
sugar. Beat until the topping holds stiff peaks.

INDEX